D1559657

The Destruction of Sodom, Gomorrah, and Jericho

Relief map of the south two-thirds of the Dead Sea between En Gedi in the
north and Hatzeva in the south. Prepared by John K. Hall, Geological Survey
of Israel, from Landsat imagery and soundings in sea. Names of sites as on
Figures 1.3 and 1.4.

The Destruction of Sodom, Gomorrah, and Jericho

Geological, Climatological, and Archaeological Background

DAVID NEEV
Geological Survey of Israel

K. O. EMERY
Woods Hole Oceanographic Institution, Massachusetts

New York   Oxford
OXFORD UNIVERSITY PRESS
1995

Oxford University Press

Oxford   New York
Athens   Auckland   Bangkok   Bombay
Calcutta   Cape Town   Dar es Salaam   Delhi
Florence   Hong Kong   Istanbul   Karachi
Kuala Lumpur   Madras   Madrid   Melbourne
Mexico City   Nairobi   Paris   Singapore
Taipei   Tokyo   Toronto

and associated companies in
Berlin   Ibadan

Copyright © 1995 by Oxford University Press, Inc.

Published by Oxford University Press, Inc.,
198 Madison Avenue, New York, New York 10016

Oxford is a registered trademark of Oxford University Press

Library of Congress Cataloging-in-Publication Data
Neev, David.
The destruction of Sodom, Gomorrah, and Jericho: geological,
climatological, and archaeological background
David Neev, K.O. Emery.
p. cm. Includes bibliographical references and index.
ISBN 0-19-509094-2
1. Geology—Dead Sea Region (Israel and Jordan)
2. Paleoclimatology—Dead Sea Region (Israel and Jordan)   3. Bible
O. T.—Antiquities.   I. Emery, K. O. (Kenneth Orris), 1914– .   II. Title.
QE319.D43N44   1995
555.694—dc20   94-38788

1 3 5 7 9 8 6 4 2

Printed in the United States of America
on acid-free paper

Preface

Humans, with their ability to think, have rationalized aspects of their environments into four successive stages: observation, understanding, prediction, and utilization. Progression through these stages has been slower for some environmental problems than for others because of lesser accessibility—such as great distance from the earth to other members of the solar system or from infrequency of events even before human presence on earth. There are numerous examples of environments that represent each stage of knowledge. Progress from stage to stage had to be slow at first, requiring oral transfer between successive "wise men," then faster, when records of thought could be passed in written form. Later progress was faster still when recognition of the value of prediction and utilization led to financial support by governments and corporations.

Among the oldest recorded observations are those of the Bible, held as oral traditions long before being written down about 2,500 years ago. Many environmental events or phenomena reached the stage of understanding only a few hundred years ago, with the advent of organized thought by scientists. An early example was Galileo's public recognition of the position of earth in the solar system, in spite of religious opposition. There are many other examples of opposition by religious leaders based on their interpretations of early texts written before understanding had progressed very far.

Progress has been relatively rapid regarding knowledge of weather patterns and climate because of their immediate importance to humans and farm crops. Even now, weather prediction must be considered an inexact science, but great improvements in weather forecasting are being made with the aid of satellite imagery and computers, which have been widely applied for less than a decade. Similarly, much effort is being devoted to earthquake prediction. Understanding of earth movements that produce earthquakes has developed during a century of observations of distribution of epicenters and their relationship to the structure of mountain ranges and faults. Knowledge of these phenomena has begun even for other rocky members of the solar system, with no immediate direct benefit to humans—an example of scientific curiosity that ultimately can have unexpected benefits.

This book was written to explore the nature of the destruction of three biblical cities—Sodom, Gomorrah, and Jericho—long before records took written form and much longer before the attention of scientists could be directed toward them. It recognizes that the cities are in an earthquake-prone belt and that their area has been subject to severe changes of climate lasting hundreds of years and capable of causing periodic immigrations to and emigrations from Israel. These events were included in stories told in ancient Israel long before their recognition as parts of natural history. Before scientific appreciation of cause and effect, geological and climatological events were attributed commonly to divine intervention by the God of Israel, meted out as punishment for sins. Elsewhere most gods and goddesses were modeled after humans. Frivolousness, for example, acceptably explained earthquakes and storms to the Greeks.

Evidence of earthquakes and climate change in the Mideast has been recognized by archaeologists, whose excavations reveal habitations as well as abandonments of settlements by successive cultures. Climate variations can be identified by changes in the remains of plants and animals as well as in soil types. The dating of many events has been made largely by radiometric methods developed only a few decades ago. These fields of science in Israel have been investigated by specialists who have published their findings and continue to apply new methods and instrumentation. Their results are available for investigators of other questions and for lay people with enough curiosity and interest to read and apply the material to related problems. We have made some of the investigations ourselves and have tried to apply results obtained by others to understanding some ancient biblical events.

Our studies of the Dead Sea region began about 35 years ago as an effort to learn how salt (sodium chloride) is deposited in lakes and seas—an initiative impelled only by scientific curiosity. Collection of water samples during monthly cruises for more than a year established the existence of a reflux flow between the shallow south basin and the deep north basin. This knowledge permitted an increased efficiency in collecting water for extracting economically valuable potassium. Samples of bottom sediments revealed prior history of rocksalt deposition and, thus, of climate during several thousand years. This information supplemented inferences derived by archaeologists from remains of settlements and changes of cultures. Other relevant geological knowledge for the region comes from the spatial and temporal distribution of earthquakes and volcanic activity that had evolved from vague ancient tradition to precise modern instrumentation. Assembly of these various kinds of information gave such promise for solving the fates of ancient Sodom and Gomorrah that we were encouraged to extend the effort to learn about the destruction of Jericho at a somewhat later date and to the legend of Noah's Flood at a much earlier date.

Perhaps other scholars will become interested in the results and wish to test and extend them to other events known from ancient tradition.

Jerusalem   D. N.
Woods Hole, Mass.   K. O. E.
December 1994

Acknowledgments

We gratefully acknowledge the hospitality and technical assistance granted by the director and staff of the Geological Survey of Israel (Ministry of Energy and Infrastructure) and by the administration of the Woods Hole Oceanographic Institution.

Archaeology and climatology are not our expertise. Close contact with professionals in these fields is needed for a multidisciplinary study. We are very much indebted to the following for personal contribution of data and critical remarks.

Archaeology: D. Allon, M. Broshi, E. Eisenberg, Y. Garfinkel, R. Gophna, I. Gilead, M. Kochavi, A. Mazar, A. Muzzolini, W. E. Rast, V. Tzaferis, Z. Vinogradov, A. Ya'akobi, A. Zertal
Climatology: J. Neumann (deceased)
Biology: Z. Bernstein, I. Dor, M. Ginzburg
Geology, Geophysics, Geochemistry, and Soil Science: Z. I. Aizenshtat, A. Almogi-Labin, E. Arieh, W. S. Broecker, Lorraine B. Eglinton, A. Frumkin, A. Gilat, D. Ginzburg, G. Goodfriend, J. K. Hall, A. Issar, E. L. Kashai, A. Kinnarti, C. Klein, Y. Levy, N. Nammeri, T. M. Niemi, Y. Nir, L. Picard, A. Shapira, J. C. Vogel, J. E. Wilson

We owe special thanks to Joy Joffrion Emery who edited the entire manuscript and reworked the last several drafts of it, computerizing and restating many sections to improve its presentation.

Contents

The Destruction of Sodom, Gomorrah, and Jericho

1

Introduction

The thrilling biblical saga of Sodom and Gomorrah leaves a deep impression on the spirit of its readers, especially the young. Basic ethical concepts such as right and wrong were dramatically portrayed by that simple and cruel, yet humane, story. Memories of even more ancient disastrous geological events apparently were interwoven into the saga. A geologist cannot remain indifferent when investigating the Dead Sea region and observing stratigraphical and structural evidence of past and continuing similar events. Forceful dynamics indicated by vertically tilted beds of rocksalt layers that have penetrated upward through the ground and by later processes that have shaped some beds into pillars trigger association with the ancient story. Such features are abundant and clearly recognizable along the foot of the diapiric structure of Mount Sedom (Arabic *Jebel Usdum*). A gas blowout during the drilling of a water well near the Amazyahu fault in 1957 only by good luck failed to produce a gush of fire and smoke. Such an event could have happened in ancient times as a natural result of faulting. Knowledge of the regional geological background permits translation of the biblical descriptions into scientific terms, which suggests that the sagas of Sodom, Gomorrah, and Jericho described real events that occurred during ancient times before much was known about geology.

Thirty-five years of the authors' professional experience in the Dead Sea region encompasses many geological aspects of the basin: deep and shallow stratigraphy, structural history, seismology, sedimentological processes, and the physical and chemical properties of the water. Archaeological studies in the region are reviewed. Although most of these studies are applicable to exploration for oil and gas or extraction of salts from brines, their results illuminate the role of changing paleogeography and paleolimnology on human environments. Climate changes and lake-level fluctuations have occurred since Mid-Pleistocene, especially during the past 50,000 years. Studies of sediments from shallow core holes delimit coastal areas that when exposed by drops in the level of the Dead Sea, quickly developed soils that could be used for agriculture. A recent speleological study of rocksalt solution by ground water in caves of Mount Sedom (Frumkin et al., 1991) using entirely different approaches and methods supplies important new data.

Archaeological data serve as environmental indicators supplementing geological data to interpret fragmentary historical (biblical) records. The manuscript deals with two main aspects. The first concerns geology and includes climatic and hydrographic perspectives. That part is extensive and is an updated review of information basic for general investigation—one of the assets of a multidisciplinary study. The second part deals with human history, including the oldest known written description of the region.

These archaeological studies indicate the chronology of cultural breaks and different cultural levels occupied by nations and tribes. Cultural breaks mean mass desertion of sites and introduction of new peoples. Many such breaks follow regional climatic changes and tectonic disturbances. These climatic changes could introduce hot dry regimes of drought and desertification in temperate subtropical areas or wet cold regimes with reduction of solar radiation, causing freezing and massive wetness of soils in northern prairies and mountainous regions. Both types of change produce chain reactions in migrations. A good example is the westward migration of the Huns that occurred in two stages during the 2nd and 4th to 5th centuries A.D.: their movement into Siberia and Russia was followed by a further invasion stressing the Goths and initiating the collapse of the Roman Empire (Encyclopedia Hebraica, 1961).

An effort to interpret physical and geographical aspects of the biblical traditions of Sodom, Gomorrah, and Jericho is a central part of this study. Similar attempts have been made during the past two thousand years and especially during the past two centuries by various scholars, pilgrims, geographers, archaeologists, and geologists. New physical data permit critical review of many previous interpretations. An example is the controversial question of just where were the "five cities of the plain." Some opinions about the sites correspond with those of other investigators but some of them differ. Unfortunately all interpretations of this subject, including this one, should be considered speculative because no ancient contemporary script or other documentary evidence has been found to enable an unequivocal identification of the sites.

Much of the study refers to the south basin of the Dead Sea (Figures 1.1, 1.2, 1.3, 1.4) where the five cities of the plain probably existed; however, the study extends beyond the actual limits of the south basin and after the dates of destruction of Sodom and Gomorrah to include the fall of Jericho. All three cities lay along the same major geological structure, the strike-slip fault that extends from the Red Sea to Turkey and whose movements affected the cultural history of sites along the entire length of that belt.

In a broad sense this study spans four different subjects: the overturning of Sodom and Gomorrah, the conquest and destruction of Jericho, the identification of sites and routes near the Dead Sea, and the story of Noah's Flood. The first three subjects were treated with great care and accuracy in the ancient descriptions, indicating that oral and later written descriptions were by people familiar with the region and with the importance of the events in the history of their people. In contrast, the physical and geographical description of the Flood is vague as though that event was much older and occurred in a more remote area so that much knowledge of it had been lost before the oral tradition was written. The subject of the Flood is included to learn whether it may have happened during one of the wet climatic phases of the Holocene.

Description in Genesis

The earliest historical description of the Dead Sea region and the plain of Sodom is that in the Bible. There are three main descriptions of the events in Sodom and Gomorrah: Genesis 13:1–13; 14:1–24; 18:16–33 and 19:1–29. These are summarized and paraphrased here for brevity and to avoid differences in some wordings and details in various translations of the Torah into the English Bible.

Genesis 13:1–13 (*Wanderings*). When Abraham and his family arrived in the Negev Desert from Ur of Chaldea the region was in the midst of a severe famine which caused him to continue on to Egypt. Later he returned to the desert and went farther northeast to Mamr'e near Hebron with his nephew Lot and their retainers. Their herds were so large that they soon decided to separate in order to avoid conflict. Lot chose to go to the well-watered plain of the Jordan, pitching his tents near Sodom.

Genesis 14:1–24 (*War of the Four Against the Five*). The kings of four Syrian cities (Shinar, Ellasar, Elam, and Goiim) defeated several kings in the Sinai and continued back north to conquer the rebellious kings of five cities in the Dead Sea region (Sodom, Gomorrah, Admah, Zeboiim, and Zoar) during a battle in the Valley of Siddim, which is the

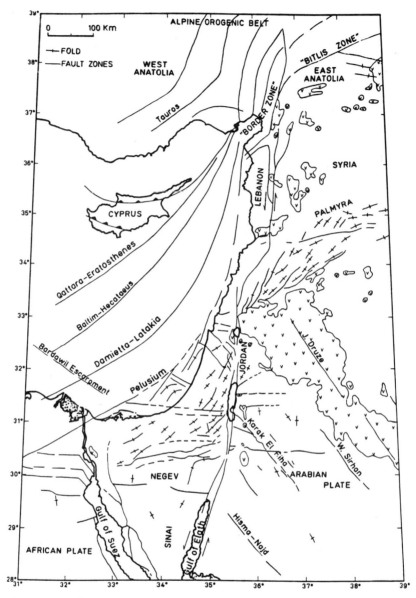

Figure 1.1. Sketch map of main tectonic elements in the east Mediterranean region. After Picard, 1970; Neev et al., 1976; Neev, Greenfield, and Hall 1985; Pictorial Archive, 1983; Kashai and Croker, 1987.

6

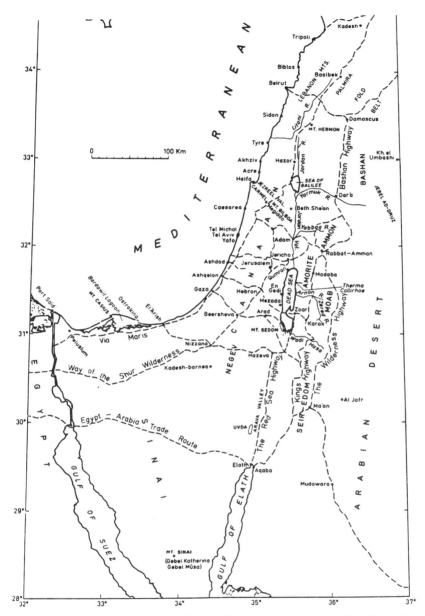

Figure 1.2. Lands southeast of the Mediterranean Sea, including the main ancient sites and travel routes.

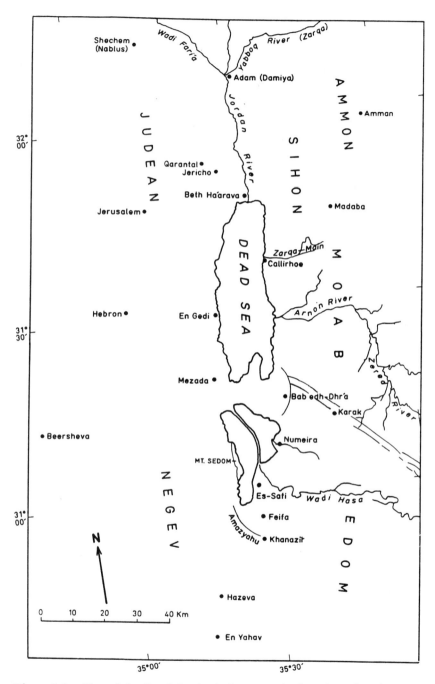

Figure 1.3. Map of the Dead Sea basin between the junction of Fari'a, Jordan, and Yabboq rivers in the north and Hazeva in the south. Note inferred location of the Zered River in the east.

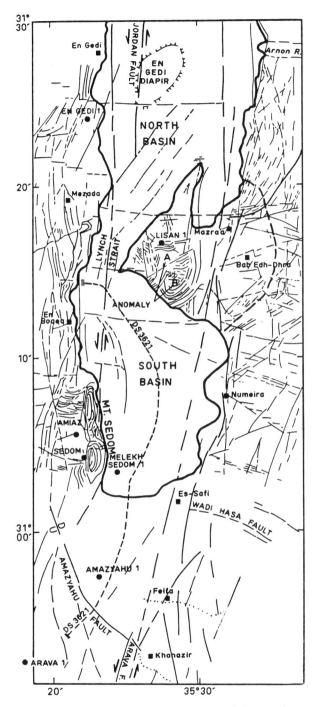

Figure 1.4. Photolineaments and reference map of the Dead Sea region between En Gedi at the north and the Amazyahu escarpment at the south. It is based on data from Nasr (1949) and the 100,000-scale merged Spot-Landsat TM (STM) satellite image of Historical Productions (1990). Also shown are

Salt Sea. The kings of Sodom and Gomorrah in their flight fell into bitumen pits that dotted this valley. The invaders took with them the defeated kings and Lot as captives, their possessions, and all the wealth and provisions of Sodom and Gomorrah. The news reached Abraham at Mamr'e, who then with his 318 retainers pursued the invaders, battled them victoriously north of Damascus and returned all people and possessions to Sodom.

Genesis 18:16–33 and 19:1–30 (*Overthrow of Sodom and Gomorrah*). The sinfulness of Sodom and Gomorrah had reached such a high level that the Lord decided to destroy them. He met Abraham at Mamr'e one afternoon to discuss the matter while two angels who had come with him continued to Sodom. On their arrival in the evening, the two were invited by Lot to spend the night in his home but the townsmen demanded homosexual access to the two visitors, who then blinded and evaded them. The next morning the angels took Lot, his wife, and two daughters away from the city with instructions to flee and not look back. They fled across the plain toward the mountains in the east but by dawn they had reached only as far as Zoar; therefore that city was spared. By then Sodom and Gomorrah and all the plain already had been overthrown and sulfurous fire destroyed these two cities, the inhabitants and the vegetation. Lot's wife looked back and was turned into a pillar of salt. Next morning Abraham looked down toward Sodom and Gomorrah and saw much smoke rising from the region.

The main environmental elements of these descriptions are the well-watered plain, the destruction of several cities in it by earthquakes, many tar pits, a rain of sulfurous fire, a pillar of salt, and the escape to Zoar, which is east at the foothills of the Moab mountains. Some direct quotations from the Bible are given in the text to confirm special parts of the inferred environment and its history.

---

crescentic fault-monocline east of and genetically related to Lisan Peninsula, diapiric structures of Mount Sedom, anomalies A and B of Lisan Peninsula, the sites of main archaeological excavations (squares), deep drill holes (large dots), and trackline of a deep seismic reflection profile along south basin.

2

General Geology

Tectonic Pattern along the Dead Sea Graben

The Dead Sea occupies a linear down-dropped region between two roughly parallel faults along the central segment of the major north-south-trending crustal rift that extends about 1,100 km from the Red Sea through the Gulf of Elath to Turkey (Figures 1.1, 1.2). This rift or geosuture separates the Arabian crustal sub-plate on the east from the Sinai one on the west. An origin as early as Precambrian (Table 2.1) is possible (Bender, 1974; Zilberfarb, 1978). Crystalline crust along the north-south trough of the Sinai sub-plate is about 40 km thick in contrast with a thickness of half as much above ridges along both flanks (Ginsburg and Gvirtzman, 1979). Toward the north the ridges appear to converge (Neev, Greenfield, and Hall, 1985). Since the Miocene period the Arabian plate has moved north about 105 km relative to the Sinai plate (Table 2.1; Quennell, 1958; Freund, 1965; Steinitz, Bartov, and Hunziger, 1978). This sort of crustal movement along either side of a rift is termed strike-slip faulting. One result of it was the opening of the Red Sea relative to the Gulf of Suez.

The Dead Sea graben, a down-dropped block between two roughly parallel faults, occupies the central segment of the long crustal rift. The boundary between these is rather sharp along the east shore of the sea (Frieslander and Ben-Avraham, 1989). Actual post-Miocene movement was along not just a single major fault but was distributed among nu-

Table 2.1 Geologic Time Scale

Eras and periods	Ages 10^6 B.P.	Dead Sea Group Formations
Cenozoic		
	0.00	
Holocene		Dead Sea
	0.01	Lisan
Pleistocene		Samra
	1.8	Amora
Pliocene		
	5	Sedom
Miocene		Hazeva
	23	
Oligocene		pre-graben
	37	
Eocene		
	55	
Paleocene		
Mesozoic		
	65	
Cretaceous		
	141	
Jurassic		
	195	
Triassic		
Paleozoic		
	230	
Permian		
	280	
Carboniferous		
	345	
Devonian		
	395	
Silurian		
	435	
Ordovician		
	500	
Cambrian		
	570	
Proterozoic		
	2600	
Archaean		

From Van Eysinga, 1975.

merous sub-parallel faults that form a 100-km-wide belt in which movements were transferred from one fault to another (Eyal et al., 1981; Gilat and Honigstein, 1981).

Recent movements have occurred along the south segment of the north-south-trending Arava fault south of the Amazyahu transverse fault (Zak and Freund, 1966). These strike-slip movements probably did not continue after Miocene along the main East fault of the Dead Sea, which is the north extension of the Arava wrench fault (Figure 1.4). In contrast, recent movements have been present along the north-northeast-trending Jordan or Dead Sea fault (Ben-Menahem et al., 1977, fig. 1). The movements extend south from east of Jericho in the north along the base of the west submarine slope of the sea and the elongate salt diapir of Mount Sedom as far as the Amazyahu fault in the south (Figure 1.4; Neev and Hall, 1979, figure 12).

The Arava and Jordan faults are parallel, both being components of the same system of lateral faults along the Dead Sea graben (Kashai and Croker, 1987). No overlap is recognizable between active strike-slip moving segments of these two faults, although an overlap is required by Girdler (1990) to generate internal rhomb-shaped basins on the floor of the graben. The genetic relationship between the different faults is not yet clearly understood (Ben-Avraham et al., 1993).

Large-scale vertical movements of several types occurred within and along the limits of the Dead Sea graben. Movements along the border faults caused the graben to subside gradually while adjoining mountain blocks were uplifted. Diapiric (upflow of plastic material) piercement by low-density rocksalt accumulations at the Lisan Peninsula, Mount Sedom, and off En Gedi caused local vertical uplifts within the graben as well as simultaneous subsidence of adjacent basins (Figures 2.1, 2.2, 2.3, 2.4). The physiographic troughs of the north and south basins separated by the sill at Lynch Strait (Figure 1.4) are believed to have been produced by this kind of tectonic movement.

Basinward sliding of accumulated sediments also occurred. The most prominent example is across the northwest-southeast-trending transverse growth fault—the Amazyahu fault escarpment beyond the south limit of the south basin (Figures 1.4, 2.3, 2.4). Similar growth or listric faults are common along the Gulf of Mexico where they have been studied thoroughly. Such faults exhibit simultaneous movement of the earth and deposition of sediments across both sides so that strata on the downthrown side are thicker than correlative strata upthrown on the side. The fault planes are nearly vertical in shallower segments, but along deeper parts the faults gradually curve and merge with nearly horizontal bedding planes. The mechanism of such movements is analogous to the enhanced gliding of a landslide where beds are lubricated by clay or rocksalt. Slippages along these planes warp the ground surface especially on the downthrown side and often are associated with earth-

Figure 2.1.   Landsat image of Lisan Peninsula showing crescentic fault-monocline at the east, Bay of Mazra'a, Bab edh-Dhr'a, and Roman roads.

quakes. Such movements may release trapped gas, oil, or water, which then can migrate up along the fault planes to reach the surface.

The lowest structures of the basement along the trough of the Dead Sea graben appear to lie beneath the Lisan Peninsula. Evidently the center of deposition in the trough has underlain the peninsula since Early Miocene. It started simultaneously with the earliest phase of subsidence of the graben and with deposition of the Hazeva Formation (Oligocene-Miocene; Figures 2.3, 2.4; Table 2.1). The depocenter stopped functioning by the end of the Sedom Formation (Pliocene) when its excessive accumulation of rocksalt caused diapiric upward movement to begin. This background updates the concept of a northward basin migration process that supposedly functioned along the trough of the Dead Sea rift since Miocene (Zak and Freund, 1981). The new interpretation is based on five sets of data:

1. The regional geological study by Folkman (1981, fig. 1, p. 144) showed the lowest Bouguer (corrected for effects of topography) gravity values in the Levant (–115 milligals) at the Lisan Peninsula, indicating a great thickness of low-density rocks.

2. A 3672-m-thick sequence of the Sedom Formation's rocksalt was drilled at Lisan #1 (Figures 1.4, 2.5) without reaching the bottom of that

Figure 2.2. Oblique aerial photograph of south basin facing south (about 1944). North-south-trending West fault escarpment of the graben is on the middle right, the 10-km-long Mount Sedom east of it, the transverse low escarpment of the Amazyahu fault farther south, and the East border fault at upper left corner.

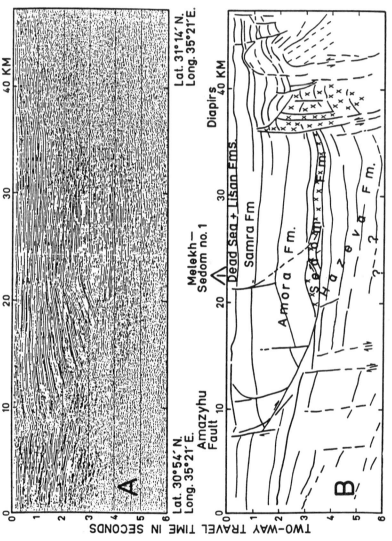

Figure 2.3. North-south longitudinal profile of the Dead Sea south basin along line DS 3621 shown in Figure 1.4. (A) Seismic profile, courtesy of the Israel National Oil Co., Ltd. (B) Geological interpretation of the seismic profile. Note absence of angular unconformities below the "shoe" of the Amazyahu listric (growth) fault along trough of the basin at about 3 seconds and upward dragging that affected all reflectors upon approaching the upward-piercing salt diapirs south of Lisan Peninsula.

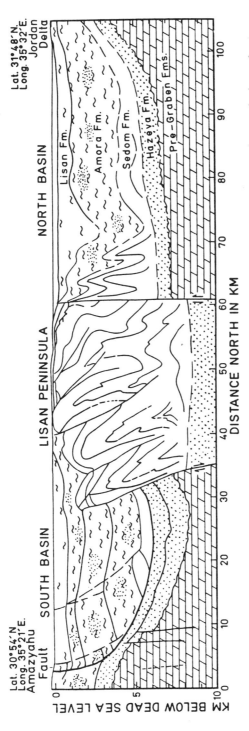

Figure 2.4. Geological section along trough of the Dead Sea from the Amazyahu fault escarpment at the south through Lisan Peninsula to the Jordan River delta and Beth Ha'arava near Jericho (Figure 1.3). Level of the Dead Sea is –400 m m.s.l. Vertical to horizontal exaggeration is 2.6. Lisan and Amora formations are marl and sand, Sedom Formation is rocksalt, Hazeva Formation is reddish sand and marl, pregraben formations are mainly dolomite.

17

unit. This site corresponds with the most negative Bouguer gravity. On a map (Figure 2.5) compiled from two surveys across the south basin and Lisan Peninsula (Nettleton, 1948; Bender, 1974), the longitudinal axis of the low-gravity features is shown to extend from south of the Amazyahu fault toward the peninsula. Closure of the lowest gravity contours farther north supports the concept that the depocenter of Sedom rocksalt is beneath the peninsula. Deepwater physiography of the north basin, southward thickening of the Pleistocene sequence along its trough, and increased diapiric uplift in the same direction (Neev and Hall, 1979) suggest that mapped values express a mirror image of the pattern found along the south basin and Lisan Peninsula. Similar conclusions are implied from results of a recent survey of the north basin by Ten Brink et al. (1993, figs. 3, 5).

3. The general outline of the sea as expressed by border faults of the graben forms a moderately curving arc convex toward the west (Frontispiece; Figure 1.4). This is superimposed on the central segment of a much longer arc that is slightly convex toward the east between the head of the Gulf of Elath (Aqaba) at the south and Mount Hermon at the north (Figure 1.2).

4. The East border fault of the Dead Sea graben forms a uniform and steep escarpment between its junction with the Amazyahu fault and the northeast corner of the sea but is structurally interrupted near the Lisan Peninsula by the Bab edh-Dhr'a curved array of flatirons and the Karak monocline (Figures 1.3, 1.4, 2.1; Neev and Emery, 1967, fig. 13). The northwest-southeast-trending graben structure of Karak-El Fiha begins at the north limit of this curved interruption near the Bay of Mazra'a, from which it extends southeast across the Jordanian plateau into the north Arabian Desert for perhaps several hundred kilometers. Basaltic intrusions having a K-Ar age of 22 million years (Steinitz and Bartov, 1992) occur between Karak and the Lisan Peninsula, suggesting a similar age for the interruption across the East border fault escarpment.

5. A unique crescentic (convex to the east) tectonic lineament branches off to the northeast from the East fault near the northeast corner of the south basin (Frontispiece; Figures 1.4, 2.1). It curves north along the contact between the foothills and the mountainous Karak-Bab edh-Dhr'a monocline, then curves slightly toward the northwest to die out before reaching the Bay of Mazra'a near the northeast corner of the peninsula (Wetzel and Morton, 1959, fig. 4). It was formed by combined effects of faulting and flexuring—a line of flatiron buttes, each of which dips steeply west and consists mostly of Cretaceous to Eocene carbonate rocks. They are overlapped by reddish sediments of the Hazeva Formation (Oligocene-Miocene), both thick and slightly tilted toward the adjacent syncline on their west. This eastward-convex crescentic fault-flatiron array is imitated on its west side by the east flank

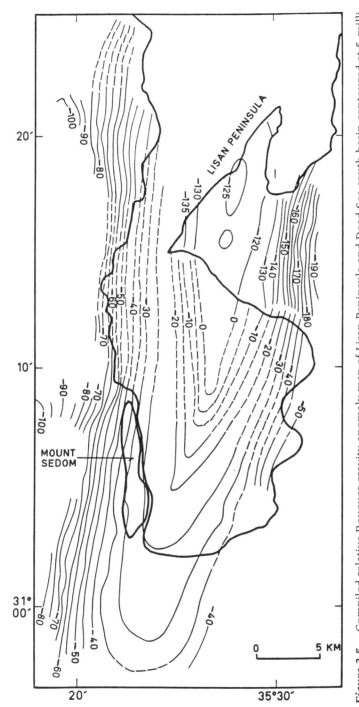

Figure 2.5. Compiled relative Bouguer gravity anomaly map of Lisan Peninsula and Dead Sea south basin contoured at 5-milli-gal intervals. Data for Lisan Peninsula are from Bender (1974, fig. 151b after an unpublished 1960 report by the Phillips Petroleum Company); data for the south basin are from Nettleton (1948). Contours from both sources are separated by a gap along the south-west shore of the peninsula. Dashed segments of contours are interpolated. Bender's map is tied to the regional net but Nettleton's values are on an arbitrary basis.

19

of a swarm of photolineaments at the southeast part of the Lisan Peninsula on the downthrown (west) side of the inferred extension of the
Dead Sea main East fault (Figures 1.4, 2.1). Apparently this is a vertically tilted sequence of layered evaporites associated with an ellipsoi-
dal salt dome named Anomaly B by Nasr (1949, p. 12). The concentration of these five different tectonic features situated on both sides of
the main border fault east of the Lisan Peninsula implies that no horizontal shift of appreciable magnitude could have occurred along that
fault of the Dead Sea graben since Miocene (Table 2.1).

Knowledge about the movement of faults that formed the Dead Sea
graben and their control over the positions of earthquakes is a major
contribution of geology to the understanding of the fates of Sodom,
Gomorrah, Jericho, and other settlements in the Dead Sea region. Without that knowledge, the inhabitants could be expected to appeal to
divine intervention especially during the long period between the destruction and its recording in written form.

General Stratigraphy and Physiography

Morphologies and rock sequences exposed on each side of the Dead Sea
graben differ appreciably. The east slope is steep (to 30°) and Precambrian crystalline rocks crop out along its base near the southeast limit
of the sea (Figures 2.1, 2.6). These basement rocks are overlain by Paleozoic to Early Mesozoic sandstones and Early to Middle Cretaceous and
Tertiary carbonates. Miocene to Recent basalts have penetrated to the
surface and are preserved on the top of the Jordanian plateau as well
as along northwest-southeast-trending tensional faults, such as the graben of Karak-El Fiha. In contrast, the west slopes (Figures 2.2, 2.7, 2.8,
2.9) are dominated by outcrops of Middle to Late Cretaceous carbonates and the crystalline basement is deeply buried under several kilometers of Paleozoic to Mesozoic carbonates, shales, and sandstones. Even
though the average slope across the West border fault zone is gentler
(7°), precipitous high cliffs are more common than along the east slope
and most were formed by faulting of Middle Cretaceous cavernous
reefoid dolomites.

Indigenous sediments of the Dead Sea Group have accumulated
within the graben since Early Miocene (Tchernov et al., 1987) and perhaps even since Oligocene when the trough began to subside tectonically. A sedimentary sequence dominated by reddish detrital stream and
lake sand, clay, and gravel deposits of the Hazeva Formation is the oldest strata of that group (Table 2.1; Figures 2.3, 2.4). The possibility that
its deposition preceded the graben is based on its wide distribution in
the north and central Negev region. These sediments were assumed to
have been deposited on a flat plain according to some geologists (Picard,
1943; Bentor and Vroman, 1957; Garfunkel and Horowitz, 1966; Steinitz

Figure 2.6. View of the distant East fault escarpment of the Dead Sea—Precambrian crystalline basement crops out along lower part of the scarp.

Figure 2.7. Escarpment along west side at En Gedi—precipitous cliffs of Cretaceous strata.

Figure 2.8. Typical West escarpment and alluvial fan north of Mezada.

Figure 2.9.   Nahal Perazim incised about 20 m into marly Lisan Formation. Note Jeep for scale.

et al.,1978; Zilberman, 1989; and A. Horowitz, 1992). Steinitz and Bartov (1992, p. 202) found no evidence of a pre-Hazeva morphologic depression in the Arava graben.

A. Horowitz (1992, p. 365) surmised that incipient rifting that formed the graben and a basin for a terminal water body within the trough of the south basin began during mid-Quaternary time. Most of the sand fraction within the Hazeva Formation was derived from Nubian sandstone (Early Cretaceous) that had been exposed to erosion by Early Neogene along both east and west sides of the rift. Although Neev (1964) and Neev and Emery (1967) agreed that the Hazeva Formation may predate the Dead Sea graben, they also noted the great thickness of that formation in the Arava #1 deep well (Figure 1.4) along the trough of the Arava Valley—more than 2,300 m as compared with the 150 m in the central Negev basins. Neev (1960, p. 6) suggested that initial stages of subsidence of the rift had occurred by Early Miocene or even Late Oligocene times and that excess detrital sediments were transported west to the Mediterranean Sea through the Beersheva-Gaza channel.

A sequence of seismic reflectors is manifest in profile DS 3621 (Figures 1.4, 2.3) beneath the deeper segment of the listric (growth) fault along the trough of the Dead Sea south basin. These reflectors are regularly layered with no large angular unconformities and extend down from below the "shoe" of the listric fault from 3.5 to 5.5 seconds (Figure 2.3A), which would be equivalent to a depth of 6 to more than 8 km. They probably represent the Hazeva Formation (Kashai and Croker, 1987). A regional seismic-stratigraphic study that ties the reflectors in Arava #1 deep hole to those in the seismic reflection profile (Figure 2.3B) indicates systematic northward thickening of that sequence toward the depocenter of the graben beneath the Lisan Peninsula (E. Kashai, personal communication). Thus, the Hazeva Formation probably belongs in the Dead Sea Group.

Sedom Formation, a Late Miocene to Pliocene rocksalt unit, unconformably overlies the Hazeva Formation. It is estimated to comprise 1,500–2,000 m of the 2,500-m-thick sedimentary sequence at Mount Sedom (Zak, 1967). Two rock types exhibit interstratified cyclic bedding—rocksalt interbedded by thin layers of anhydrite and gypsum, reddish dolomite, silt, and clay. Rocksalt composes about 75% of the Sedom Formation. Most of the sodium chloride and potassium chloride originally was derived from marine brines that had reached the graben from the Mediterranean and Red seas. Connections of the Dead Sea region with these seas were interrupted during Pliocene and Pleistocene by tectonic rise of sills across the Jezreel and Arava Valleys.

Gravels, sands, clays, marls, chalks, as well as beds of rocksalt from recycled brines, were deposited in lakes within the graben. In the Dead Sea Group these sediments are known as the Amora, Samra, Lisan, and Dead Sea formations (Figures 2.3, 2.4, 2.10; Table 2.1). Detrital materi-

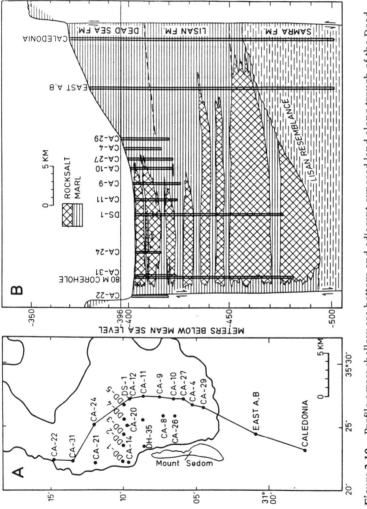

Figure 2.10. Profile across shallow sea bottom and adjacent exposed land along trough of the Dead Sea south basin. (A) Positions of CA and DD corehole series, the 74-m-deep Dead Sea #1, the 80-m-deep hole (same site as corehole CA-31), east A, B (161-m-deep hole), and Caledonia 285-m-deep corehole. Track of the shallow geological cross-section also is shown. (B) Geological cross-section of Holocene to late Mid-Pleistocene sedimentary sequence composed of the following formations and rock types: Dead Sea and Lisan formations—alternating layers of rocksalt and Lisan type marl as well as unlaminated sandy layers, an unnamed formation dominated by rocksalt deposited during late Mid-Pleistocene or Riss-Würm interglacial stage, and the Late to Mid-Pleistocene Samra Formation that lithologically resembles the Lisan Formation but was deposited during the Riss glacial stage.

26

als derived from weathering of older rocks cropping out in the catchment area were deposited on floors of lakes in the rift valley by processes similar to those still functioning.

Type locality of the Amora Formation is at outcrops that surround the Mount Sedom diapir where its thickness exceeds 400 m (Zak, 1967). It is dominated by whitish-yellowish to brown gypsiferous marls and chalks and is subdivided into five members on the basis of difference in abundance of accessory strata such as conglomerate, sandstone, or rocksalt. This formation thickens basinward to several thousand meters (Figures 2.3, 2.4).

The Samra Formation was described by Bentor (1960, p. 100) as "a fluvio-limnic sequence up to 25 m thick, consisting of fine-grained partly calcareous sandstone and silt, oolitic chalk and limestone, calcareous finely bedded shales, green clays, as well as conglomerates and breccias, mainly of flint and limestone fragments . . . The Samra Formation overlies unconformably the . . . Hazeva Formation or else older strata . . . [and] is overlain with slight angular unconformity by the Lisan Formation." Picard (1943) described its type locality 7 km north-northeast of Jericho as well as other outcrops in the Jordan Valley. Bentor and Vroman (1957) described its outcrops in the northern Arava.

Zak (1967) incorporated sediments of the Samra Formation as the upper member (Ams) of the Amora Formation whereas Begin, Ehrlich, and Nathan (1974) considered it to be an alluvial fan facies of the basal member in the Lisan Formation. $^{230}Th^{234}U$ ages from columnar sections along the west flanks of Samra Lake indicate that its time-span commenced before 350,000 B.P. and continued to about 63,000 B.P. (Kaufman, Yechieli, and Gardosh, 1992). A substantial hiatus between Samra and the overlying Lisan Formation is inferred from these results. Ionic ratios in Samra sediments suggest a resemblance to brines of the Dead Sea (Gardosh, 1987). During its last phase Samra Lake receded from its highest level of about −180 to −400 m mean sea level (m.s.l.).

Characteristic alternating finely laminated white aragonitic chalks and dark gray detrital marls dominate the Lisan Formation, a Late Pleistocene sequence that accumulated between 60,000 and 11,000 B.P. Possibly the Recent (post-Lisan) Dead Sea Formation defined here for the first time should have been included within the Lisan Formation as a member deposited during a time less pluvial (drier) than that of the Lisan. The Lisan marl thins toward the former shores along the border faults (Figure 2.11). Where thick marls are exposed to stream erosion, they are capable of standing as high cliffs (Figures 2.9, 2.12, 2.13, 2.14) but are unstable.

The Dead Sea, being a terminal body, has no outflow. All sediments that reach the depositional plains of its two basins are trapped there and no erosional unconformities are expected. Since Late Pliocene the floor of the south basin has been at a higher elevation than that of the north

Figure 2.11. Whitish Lisan Lake sediments filling valley of Nahal Zohar northwest of Mount Sedom and onlapping the Middle Cretaceous dolomites across West border fault escarpment. Horizontal lines beyond it are lake terraces or shorelines that reach an elevation of -180 m m.s.l. Roman fortress at trough of wadi-guarded ancient road west to Judea and Gaza.

Figure 2.12. Repetitive slump structures of unconsolidated Lisan sediments caused by earthquakes and subsidence. Interformational asymmetric basinward folding is well exhibited within Nahal Perazim west of Mount Sedom.

Figure 2.13. Jordan River north of Adam (Damiya) Bridge is deeply entrenched into soft marls of the Lisan and Samra formations. This site is 30 km south of the sill between Beth She'an and the Dead Sea basins at Tel Naqra. Height of cliffs is about 80 m above the Jordan bed—an obvious source of landslides that temporarily could have dammed the river flow down to Jericho and the Dead Sea.

Figure 2.14. Shallow ford of the Jordan River at Beth Ha'arava (Figure 1.3). Joshua and the Israelites may have crossed here to attack Jericho. Just north of this site Christ was baptized.

basin, so hiatuses due to nondeposition are present within sediments of the south basin. These hiatuses are at the top of salt layers precipitated during ends of climatic cycles—drying phases when the sea level dropped below the floor of Lynch Strait, the sill that separates the two basins (Figure 1.4). At these low levels the south basin is cut off from brine and becomes a completely desiccated playa. At the same time the water or brine body of the north basin is preserved but at lower elevations. Some clay, together with rocksalt and apparently bittern salts, continues to be deposited.

Renewals of wet climate allowed marls similar to the Lisan facies—alternating laminated aragonitic and detrital materials—to be the first sediments deposited from diluted brines. Common in the south basin they unconformably overlie rocksalt layers of the previous cycle. Complete records of the entire sedimentary sequence of the Dead Sea Group should have been preserved beneath the present floor of the north basin. Climatic changes during post-Miocene time must have left their record as facies changes in sediments of both basins.

An estimate of average rate of deposition within the central part of the south basin was made by J. E. Wilson (personal communication) for most of the sequence of the Dead Sea Group. The top of the Miocene Hazeva Formation correlates with the seismic reflection basement at an acoustic depth of about 3.6 seconds, about 6,300 m assuming an average acoustic velocity of 2,000 m/second on the longitudinal deep reflection profile (Figure 2.3A). During the 5 million years (Table 2.1) since the end of Miocene, the average rate of sediment accumulation would have been 1.3 mm per year. Seismic-physiographic affinities of that profile suggest that the average rate of sedimentation equaled the rate of tectonic subsidence of the basin during most of that period.

Similar rates of deposition were estimated by Neev (1964, p. 136) for the 10-m-thick sequence of the Dead Sea Formation during the Holocene (the past 10,000 years) in the south and central parts of the south basin where marly sediments dominate (corehole CA-27, Figure 2.10). Neev and Emery (1967, pp. 20, 85) obtained a rate of 1 mm per year for the 10-cm-thick layer of laminated white aragonitic and dark calcitic sediments that accumulated on the floor of the south basin during the past 100 years, as well as encrusting trunks of trees drowned more than 100 years ago during the latter part of the latest transgression of the sea. An appreciably greater rate ten times or perhaps even more was estimated by Neev and Hall (1979, p. 234) for the Holocene sequence across the north half of the "abyssal plain" of the north basin, where there is a northward thickening sedimentary wedge at the subsea Jordan River delta. Such an estimate is highly speculative because the age of the lower reflector of that wedge is ill-defined and practically nothing is known about acoustic velocities in these seismic units.

Presence of hydrocarbons in reservoir rocks buried within the sedimentary fill of the graben is indicated by two types of occurrences. Seepages of heavy oil residues such as asphalt and ozokerite devoid of light volatile components occur mostly along the bases of both West and East fault escarpments. Their origin is probably in bituminous rocks within the pregraben Late Cretaceous sedimentary sequence now deeply buried under the sloping Dead Sea Group (Figures 2.15, 2.16). Gas occurs in shallow drill holes within the south basin near the Amazyahu fault escarpment (Figures 1.4, 2.3). Light oil could have been associated with that gas. Some makes its way upward along faults and joints produced by seismic activity (Figure 2.17). Sandstone dikes and mass movements in freshly deposited sediments such as those of Lisan marl are revealed by interformational folding (Figure 2.12). They are typical products of earthquakes affecting soft sediments.

This discussion of the various kinds of sediment deposited in the Dead Sea region and their variations that accompanied changes in climate and effects of tectonism long before human history began provides background for understanding the causes of later changes during early human habitation of the same region. Without such knowledge even most modern viewers are likely to give little attention to the sedimentary strata and even less to the information about climate that the sediments can provide.

Affinities of the Sodom and Gomorrah Earthquakes

The many faults in the Dead Sea region and their continued activity are illustrated by concentration of earthquake epicenters in the region. Positions of only the more destructive shocks between 1907 and 1993 having magnitudes of 4.0 to 6.9 on the Richter scale are denoted by Figure 2.18. If numerous minor shocks as low as magnitude 2.0 had been included, a concentrated line of epicenters between the mouth of the Gulf of Elath through the Dead Sea to north Lebanon would be displayed. Application of modern techniques for identification of soil disturbances by past earthquakes, a form of paleoseismology (Adams, 1982), probably would reveal evidences of many ancient earthquakes in the region.

Three factors control most effects of an earthquake at a given site: distance of the epicenter from the site, frequency-magnitude relations, and physical characteristics of the subsurface such as rock density, mineralogy, matrix-to-coarse-detritus ratio, compaction, and liquification-slide processes. Ben-Menahem et al. (1977) and Ben-Menahem (1981) considered that magnitude of the Sodom and Gomorrah earthquake was more than 7.0 on the Richter scale somewhere along the Dead Sea rift. It may have been the strongest earthquake in this region during the 6,000 years of historical time. Biblical description of this event, the sole source of eyewitness information, was only an oral tradition for several thousand years.

Figure 2.15. Photograph of the West escarpment south of Dead Sea. Upper Cretaceous limestones and marls have been warped downward to the east where they were deeply buried under later thick sediments of the graben.

Figure 2.16. Sequence of small terraces north of Mount Sedom formed at successive elevations due to changing levels of Lisan Lake and the sea. These are indicators of climatic changes.

Figure 2.17. Sandstone dike through Lisan marl at Nahal Parazim (near area shown in Figure 2.9) west of Mount Sedom. Such dikes are common effects of large earthquakes on unconsolidated sediments.

Perhaps some characteristics of the 1985 earthquake at Mexico City (Munich Reinsurance Co., 1986) can help construct a working hypothesis for the nature of the Sodom and Gomorrah earthquake. The epicenter of this earthquake was more than 350 km from the city, off the Pacific coast of Mexico at the junction between the Pacific and American tectonic plates. Mexico City was built on a basin containing thick lake sediments bordered by faulted elongate mountain ranges of dense rocks. The sequence of sediments has a resonant vibration period of 1 to 3 seconds allowing it to act like an amplifier for earthquake waves having that frequency. Shock waves within the basin were intensified by a factor of 5 to 20 and affected the city as though it were on a bowl of jelly. Most of the city shook with each new wave, increasing oscillations of buildings until final limits were exceeded and they collapsed. Accelerations ranged from 1% of gravity at the edge of the basin to 20% in the city center so that only structures built at the flanks on dense rocks were well preserved.

Similar effects of thick soft sediments have been noted in earthquakes of California, many times in the Los Angeles basin of southern California, especially in 1994, and the Loma Prieta quake in 1989 that caused much destruction in San Francisco 90 km distant from its epicenter. The triggering and physical nature of the Sodom and Gomorrah event long ago could have been analogous. It is not necessary for the epicenter of the earthquake that shook the plain of Sodom to have been within the Dead Sea basin itself. The epicenter of that ancient earthquake may have been associated with strike-slip movement along one of the rift's many faults, perhaps hundreds of kilometers from the south basin. In this specific event destructive effects of amplified resonance in basin fill, a gliding effect of the downthrown side along the northeast side of the Amazyahu growth fault, and sudden release of pressures caused by outburst of inflammable gases could have been simultaneous to produce an especially impressive display.

Hydrogeology

Marine transgressions that brought seawater to the Dead Sea rift occurred during Late Tertiary (Bentor, 1961; Zak, 1967). Much of their load of dissolved salts was deposited in secondary troughs along the two routes of water flow toward the Dead Sea—in the Gulf of Elath and Arava Valley and in the Jezreel and Jordan valleys, including the Sea of Galilee. Brines from these sources percolated through reservoir rocks in the adjacent mountains where their great density caused some to remain trapped within lower parts of these bodies. Small amounts of dissolved salts derived from weathering of adjacent rocks were added to these oceanic brines. After cessation of oceanic inflow sometime during Pliocene or Early Pleistocene, these brines were recycled sev-

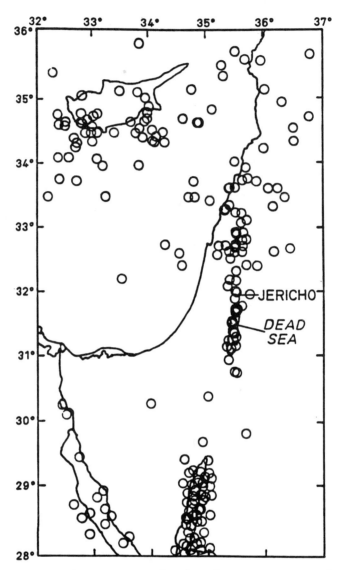

Figure 2.18. Distribution pattern of earthquake epicenters in Israel and the easternmost Mediterranean Sea (Richter magnitude of 4.0 to 6.9). Compiled by Seismological Division of the Israel Institute of Petroleum Research and Geophysics for the period 1907 to 1993 indicating greatest activity along the Elath–Dead Sea–Jordan rift (A. Shapira, personal communication). Similar patterns are shown by compilations for other time spans (Arieh and Rotstein, 1985, fig. 3; Rotstein and Arieh, 1986, fig. 2; Girdler, 1990, fig. 1; Van Eck and Hoffstetter, 1990, fig. 2).

eral times within the rift, a process that was initiated and maintained mostly because of climatic changes.

During pluvial (wet or glacial) epochs, excessive quantities of flood waters drained toward the Dead Sea from the catchment area that extends from Mount Hermon in Syria at the north to east Sinai and Negev and Edom mountains at the south (Figures 1.2, 1.3). Some of these waters reached the terminal body but much accumulated in mountainous reservoirs above denser brines. Increased pressures caused some to be forced upward along the graben's border faults, from which they escaped as saline springs and drained toward the terminal body. This model was corroborated by data from observation wells at the Sea of Galilee after the extremely rainy season of 1969 (Neev, 1978). During the same pluvial epochs, denser brines already present in the sea were being diluted by inflowing fresh water. Rising water of that sea eventually transgressed upstream to mix with fresh waters of intermediate lakes. Some newly formed brackish waters penetrated into mountainous reservoir rocks to be stored there as water layers according to their densities. During the next stage of falling levels, these waters drained back into the sea.

Water Stratification within the
Lisan Lake–Dead Sea System

Seasonal stratification within monomictic lakes—those with complete annual overturn—is the most common structure in water bodies after the melting of ice in springtimes. Semipermanent stratification forms in meromictic lakes—those with only partial overturn—mostly during pluvial climates when large quantities of fresh water are being added and levels are rising. Theoretically a structure of more than two stratified water masses can form within a lake if changes occur at intervals during a time of increasing pluviality. Later the stratification within such a lake can be destroyed if its level is lowered by excessive rates of evaporation.

Neev and Emery (1967) detected and studied the most recent occurrence of semipermanent water stratification in the Dead Sea. During Byzantine time the level had dropped drastically to –436 m m.s.l., then began to rise again nearly 1,000 years ago to form the Upper Water Mass and reach the level of –400 m m.s.l. about 300 years ago. During this low stand, halite (rocksalt) was deposited and accumulated at the bottom of the north basin to plaster its slopes below the –436 m m.s.l. depth contour (436 m below mean sea level of the Mediterranean or open ocean), nearly 40 m below the 1956 Dead Sea level. An increase in runoff-to-evaporation ratio followed, as indicated by the presence of more dilute brine in the Upper Water Mass than in the Lower Water Mass and by accumulation of a few decimeters thickness of dark gray marl above rocksalt on the sea floor. In this way the gradual rise of surface level marked the beginning of a new climatic or pluvial epoch.

In a more recent study Levy (1984) considered that the halite layer in the north basin was deposited sometime between 1045 and 270 B.P. with an average date of 600 B.P. This date estimate is based on rate of deposition of marly sediments accumulated on top of the layer through-out the entire basin, as well as on radiocarbon age of aragonite precipi-tated between halite crystals in one sample. Stiller and Chung (1984) estimated an age of about 300 B.P. for that halite according to the rate of radium accumulation in the Upper Water Mass since beginning of the meromictic structure. The sea reached its peak level of –391 m m.s.l. near the end of the 19th century, after which a steady-state condition lasted until 1932 with less uniform levels until 1952 (Ashbel, 1951; Klein, 1986). Accumulation of the Upper Water Mass isolated the Lower Water Mass and detached it from the atmosphere. As a result dissolved oxygen was consumed and disappeared from the Lower Mass. New supplies of dissolved salts could not reach the latter except perhaps for small quantities from submarine springs. Consequently deposition of rocksalt ceased even though brines of this fossil water mass still were saturated with sodium chloride. Seasonally during early springs a more dilute water layer formed above the Upper Water Mass, initiating an internal stratum. During early autumn this seasonal stratification was destroyed mostly by cooling at the surface and by mixing through more intense winds and currents. An overturn occurred down to the inter-face with the Lower Water Mass at –436 m m.s.l. so that the Upper Water Mass of that meromictic sea temporarily behaved like a normal mono-mictic lake.

Lowering of the Dead Sea has continued since 1932, although in-terrupted by intervals of more or less steady-state levels (Figure 2.19). The level dropped to –395 m m.s.l. between 1932 and 1936 and again almost to –399 between 1955 and 1964. It then fluctuated upward to –398 m m.s.l. until 1972 when the drop was renewed almost uninter-ruptedly, reaching –408 m m.s.l. in 1988 (Steinhorn and Assaf, 1980; Klein, 1986; Anati and Stiller, 1991—all based on measurements by the Dead Sea Works).

Recent mixing of the entire water body probably began about 1956 and proceeded in stages to end in 1979. It was genetically related to falling levels of the sea surface though it lagged behind by a few years (Figure 2.19). The vertical mixing process was expressed by the falling level of the density surface that separates the Upper Water Mass from the underlying Intermediate and Lower water masses (Neev and Emery, 1967). These changes were traced by measurements of several param-eters along the water column: *in situ* temperature, density, total salinity, and average concentration of major ions and tritium. The values were documented by Neev (1964, figs. III-16, 17—single measurements for

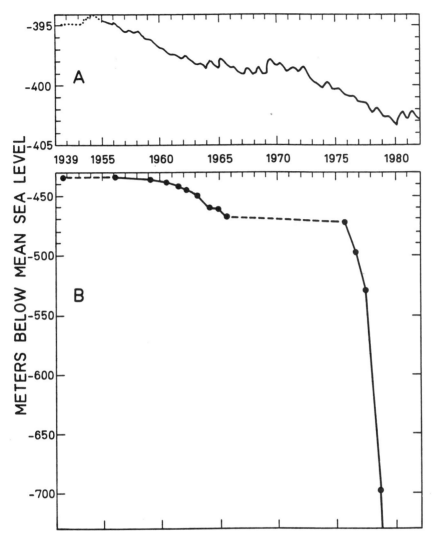

Figure 2.19. Diagrams expressing the mixing process of the Dead Sea water body between 1956 and 1979: (A) Dropping levels of surface of the Dead Sea (–396 to –402.6 m m.s.l.). (B) Dropping levels of the pycnoclines-thermoclines that separate Upper (mixed) Water Mass from Intermediate Water Mass and the latter from underlying Lower (fossil) Water Mass, –436 m m.s.l. in 1960 to greatest depth of the Dead Sea, –730 m m.s.l. in 1979.

1939 and 1956); Neev and Emery (1967—monthly measurements for the period April 1959 to July 1960); Nissenbaum (1969—for 1963 to 1965); Ben-Avraham, Hanel, and Assaf (1977—for October 1975); Beyth (1980—for August 1974 to March 1977); Steinhorn and Assaf (1980—for 1975 to 1977), and Steinhorn (1985—for 1975 to 1979). A few bathythermograph measurements were made by Neev between 1961 and 1967. The depth distribution of pycnometric (water density) values plotted in Figure 2.19 indicate that the long-lasting—several hundred years—interface between Upper and Intermediate water masses at –436 m m.s.l. started to deteriorate in 1956 signaling the start of a complete vertical mixing process.

The rate of post-1956 mixing increased and gained momentum until mid-1965 when the pycnocline reached a level of –470 m m.s.l.—a drop of about 35 m (note that the vertical scale of Figure 2.19B is ten times larger than that of Figure 2.19A). As long as the south basin contained a few meters depth of Dead Sea waters, bottom currents of hot dense brines flowed north through Lynch Strait (Figure 1.4). On reaching the deep north basin, these bottom currents wedged in as density currents at and above the –436 m m.s.l. interface, somewhat eroding the top of the Intermediate Water Mass.

Before 1956 the yearly mixing event of the Upper Water Mass was equivalent to early to midwinter overturns of monomictic lakes. Vertical mixing of the entire water body followed a systematic decrease in runoff-to-evaporation ratio since 1955 that produced a gradual increase in salinity of the Upper Water Mass to the stage where its density equaled that of the underlying mass. The depth of vertical mixing or partial overturning reached during each stage was determined by water densities of brines at the sea surface and at depth.

Validity of the mixing process between Upper and Intermediate water masses during 1956 to 1965 is corroborated by prominent increased concentrations recorded for magnesium, potassium, and chloride with a decrease of sodium ions, as well as by decrease of the sodium to chloride ratio in the Upper Water Mass for that period. These changes could not have occurred as a result of halite (NaCl) precipitation because no accumulation of such deposits was observed at the sea bottom and because of the low degree of halite supersaturation in brines of both masses during that time. Values of these factors in the Upper Water Mass were halite saturation of 0.71 and total dissolved solids of 305.6 g/l instead of 1.0 to 1.15 and 330 to 340 g/l required to start the precipitation process (Beyth, 1980, p. 156 and tables 13-l, 13-2).

It is unfortunate that few bathythermograph measurements were made between 1965 and 1975. A stage of mild mixing of the Dead Sea water body probably already had begun in 1956, nearly reaching the critical point of total overturn in 1965 (Figure 2.19B; Beyth, 1980, tables 13-1 to 13-6). Completion of that process could have occurred within a few years if the dry climate of late 1950s and early 1960s had continued. That process was delayed until 1973 because large quantities of fresh water were supplied to the system during two sets of rainy years between 1963 and 1972. The final mixing of the entire water body occurred between 1975 and early 1979 as described by Steinhorn (1985). It lagged two to three years behind the renewed drop in surface level.

Complete overturn of the sea between 1956 and 1979 was vigorously accelerated by an artificial factor—man-caused diversion into agriculture of most freshwater resources of the catchment areas. Before 1964 nearly all freshwaters had flowed freely into the sea.

The importance here of these modern studies of Dead Sea waters is in examining how climatic changes may have influenced its salinity and water levels during past thousands of years. This allows evaluation of some effects on coastal settlements and agriculture at the time of Sodom, Gomorrah, and other sites. These controls by the sea may have been more critical than those of raids by hungry neighbors.

3

Climate Inferred from Geology and Archaeology

Stratigraphy and Climate since Late Pleistocene

Sediments of the South Basin

Early climatic interpretations for the Lisan and later formations (Late Pleistocene and Holocene—Neev and Emery, 1967, figs. 16, 17) were supported and updated by information from additional coreholes. Although most new and old coreholes (Figure 2.10) bottomed at relatively shallow depths, 20 to 30 m, four of them reached greater depths, 74, 80, 161, and 285 m beneath the 1960 floor of the Dead Sea south basin. The sequences consist of alternating layers of marl and rocksalt. Most marls were deposited from dilute brine during high lake levels and contain alternating laminae of chemical deposits of white aragonite, gray gypsum, and fine-grained detritus consisting of yellowish, brown, green, or dark gray carbonates, quartz, and clay. The detrital fraction is coarser and more dominant toward the deltas, especially near Amazyahu escarpment in the south. Rocksalt layers indicate deposition from more concentrated brine when the levels dropped to about –400 m m.s.l. Lower elevations could have been reached when the sea continued to shrink and when the runoff-to-evaporation ratio diminished, bringing the south basin to complete dessication. As neither the geochemical nature (ionic ratios) of the brines nor the physiography of the terminal water body has changed at least since Late Pleistocene or Lisan Lake time (Katz, Kolodny, and Nissenbaum, 1977), it is probable that through

44

the past 60,000 years rocksalt was precipitated only when the water surface was at or below the critical level of –400 m m.s.l.

Gamma-ray logs for some of the new coreholes (Figures 2.10, 3.1, 3.2) provide more objective and precise depths of marl and rocksalt layers than do actual samples of sediments. Content of radiogenic minerals in the rocksalt is negligible compared with that in the marl; thus, these layers identify changing physical environments and climates as well as correlating stratigraphy. On gamma-ray logs the peaks or highest intensities of positive anomalies indicate that marl layers or wet climatic subphases and their thicknesses on the logs are proportional to their duration. Presence of negative anomalies or very low levels of gamma radiation show both the existence and thickness of rocksalt layers that denote dry climatic phases. Time relationships or durations between wet and dry phases are not directly proportional to thickness ratios of relevant layers since marl and rocksalt have different rates of deposition. A complete record of climatic history can be found only in coreholes within the trough of a basin where more or less continuous deposition has occurred and not along its periphery where there may be hiatuses in the record, especially for the south basin at levels higher than –400 m m.s.l..

Core samples from drill holes and samples from outcrops along the periphery of the south basin vaguely correlate with prominent acoustic reflectors in records of shallow-penetration seismic surveys across both south and north basins (Ben-Avraham et al., 1993). These results were incorporated with those of geological, radiologic, and environmental-cultural or archaeological studies made along the Dead Sea–Jordan rift. These sources provided data for diagrams of the general climatic, lithologic, and physiographic history of the region during the Holocene. Most important here, sedimentary sequences of alternating rocksalt and marl layers across the whole basin are an efficient means for learning climate changes at the time of Sodom and Gomorrah as well as for stratigraphic correlations.

Mount Sedom Cave Studies

A new speleological study of karstic caves within the Mount Sedom rocksalt diapir (Figures 1.4, 3.3, 3.4) yielded additional information on climatic changes during the past 7,000 years (Frumkin et al., 1991). Even though this approach and the nature of data recovered from the caves differ from those of the coreholes, agreement between patterns of the two climatic interpretations is remarkable.

During times of higher levels of the sea or during wetter colder climatic phases, some floodwaters of Mount Sedom's catchment area drained into fissures in the rocksalt and dissolved their way down to form vertical karstic shafts or chimneys. These waters dropped to ele-

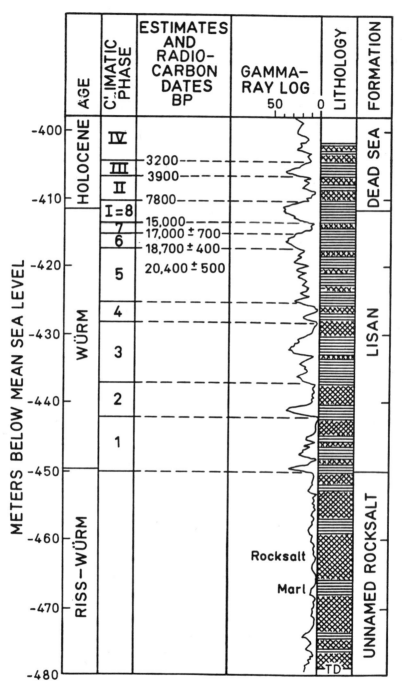

Figure 3.1. Composite log of continuous gamma-ray measurements and interpreted lithologic descriptions of an 80-m-deep hole in the northwest part of the south basin near CA-31 corehole. Climatic phases 1 to 8 are latest Pleistocene and I to IV are Holocene. The gamma-ray log accurately expresses alternating lithologic characteristics (rocksalt versus marl).

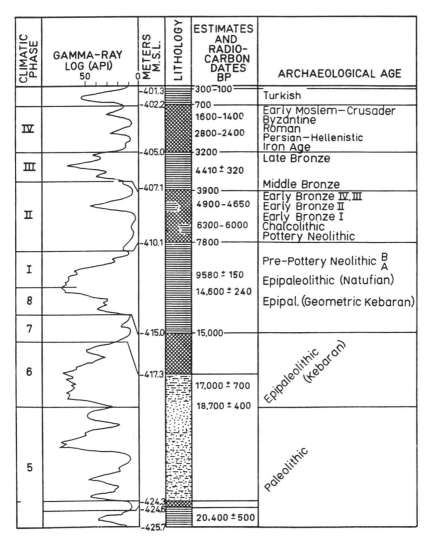

Figure 3.2. Composite log of the nearly 25-m sedimentary sequence at DD-1 corehole about 3 km north of Mount Sedom's north plunge (Figure 2.10A) within the Dead Sea south basin. The log includes continuous gamma-ray measurements, lithologic description, results of radiocarbon analyses and interpreted division into climatic phases and correlation with changing cultural ages. Original lithologic log was supplemented by that of corehole CA-14 drilled a few years earlier 0.5 km farther south in which better sampling techniques produced more reliable lithologic descriptions. Minor thickness variations of different layers are illustrated by gamma-ray and lithologic logs. Plotted radiocarbon ages represent just approximate values. Age estimates of climatic phases are more reliable based on better established archaeological boundaries.

vations within the diapir near the sea level, then seeped east to produce subhorizontal galleries that ended at the seashore as cave mouths.

Outlets of the caves occur at various elevations in accordance with
past changed levels of the Dead Sea. Some are high above the present
level, representing specific wet phases of climate. Longitudinal profiles
of some galleries indicate that immature segments have east gradients
as steep as 30° but more mature ones have gentler slopes. Diameters of
subhorizontal galleries formed during pluvial periods are larger than
those of interpluvials according to the intensity of floodwater flowing
through them. An average uplift rate of 1 mm with a maximum of
3.5 mm per year was computed for the diapir during Holocene (Zak,
1967); these values were included by Frumkin et al. (1991) in calcula-
tions of Dead Sea paleolevels.

Paleobotanical analyses were made on driftwood swept by floodwaters through the chimneys into the caves and deposited with detrital
sediments in galleries at different elevations. Samples of these driftwood
fragments were analyzed for their radiocarbon ages in order to establish the chronology of Dead Sea water levels and for botanical composition to identify climates during the time that the wood grew.

Integration of results from the Mount Sedom speleological study
with those from the south basin corehole stratigraphy is instructive
because the two complement each other. Cave data show the chronology of highest elevations reached by the water during climatic wet
phases, whereas the corehole data determine the dates of low levels
during dry phases. The presence of much higher levels than at present
is shown not only by Mount Sedom cave sediments but also by numerous small terraces or beach levels on the more gently sloping parts of
the bordering areas as illustrated by Figures 2.11 and 2.16.

Radiocarbon Dates

Evaluations of radiocarbon dates for samples from Lisan and Dead Sea
cores as well as for those from Mount Sedom and nearby archaeological sites (Table 3.1) raise questions regarding the validity of the radiocarbon method for determining precise chronology, at least in Dead Sea
environments. Some causes of anomalies are understood and empiri-
cal correction factors can be introduced. An example is the effect of dead
carbon brought in solution or in suspension to the sea where it con-
taminated recent sediments, producing erroneous older apparent ages
(Neev and Emery, 1967, p. 69). Another set of problems comes from
disseminated organic carbon in south basin sediments, some yielding
ages apparently too young for which no explanation can yet be provided. Both organic carbon and carbonate carbon were analyzed in five
of the eight samples of Table 3.1. The results indicate differences in
vertical distributions of the two sets of ages. Good control over relative

Figure 3.3. Lot's Wife at Mount Sedom—a narrow and tall joint block having a rectangular cross-section. It consists of rocksalt layers vertically tilted and forced up into the floor of Lisan Lake so that their top became dissolved to form a salt-table before deposition of a cap of gypsiferous Lisan marl (Gary, McAfee, and Wolf, 1974).

Figure 3.4. A vadose chimney in rocksalt at the top of Mount Sedom overlain by Lisan marl.

Table 3.1 Radiocarbon Dates for Carbonate Carbon and Disseminated Organic Carbon in Corehole Samples from the Dead Sea South Basin

Sample no.	Depth m m.s.l.	Corehole and sample no.	Lab. symbol and no.	Radiocarbon dates B.P. Carbonate	Organic carbon	Percent dry matter (E.O.M.)
1	-403	CA-27 (US-2)	R 661/1		4410 ± 320	0.5 to 1.0
2	-406	DD-3 (B-1, 50)	Pta 5680 / Pta 5698	8750 ± 70	2630 ± 80	1.3
3	-410	CA-27 (US-3)	R 661/2		9580 ± 150	0.5 to 1.0
4	-419	DD-5 (B-4, 16)	Pta 5682 / Pta 5781	13,810 ± 110	4030 ± 110	0.13
5	-419.7	DD-2 (B-3, 2)	Pta 5668 / Pta 5691	20,800 ± 220	5330 ± 100	1.32
6	-420	CA-14	L-735 M / L-735 M	18,700 ± 400	<300	0.25
7	-425	CA-14	L-735 N	20,400 ± 500		
8	-428	DD-1 (B-5, 12)	Pta 5660 / Pta 5671	16,800 ± 170	7310 ± 90	3.32

Laboratory symbols: R = T. A. Rafter, Wellington, New Zealand; Pta = J. C. Vogel, CSIR, Pretoria, South Africa; L- = W. S. Broecker, Lamont Geological Observatory, Palisades, N.Y., United States.

ages is provided by correlations of alternating rocksalt and marl sequences in the nearly horizontal layers of the east-west cross section of the south basin as indicated by gamma-ray logs for the five coreholes (DD-1 to DD-5; Figures 2.10 and 3.5).

Radiocarbon age analyses were made by three laboratories having high standards, so inconsistencies in apparent ages cannot be placed on analytical techniques but apparently are caused by factors not yet understood. Extreme differences in ages for different materials, such as in sample 6 of Table 3.1, are known to have occurred elsewhere. For example, analyses made by the same laboratory on samples from opposite ends of the same stick (1 m long and 3 cm diameter) from an Early Bronze I chamber tomb excavated at Bab edh-Dhr'a yielded ages of about 5100 B.P. and zero (D. Ortner of the Smithsonian Institution, personal communication). Similar doubts were raised by Weinstein

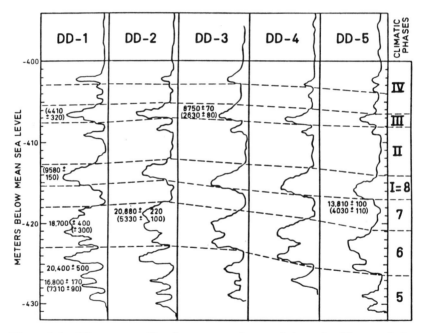

Figure 3.5. West-east profile of gamma-ray logs made in each of five coreholes DD-1 to DD-5 across the Dead Sea south basin (Figure 2.10A). Correlation between the five lithologic sequences is good, and integration of climatic phases during latest Pleistocene (5 to 8) and Holocene (I to IV) as intepreted in this profile is considered reliable. Results of radiocarbon analyses made on sedimentary samples recovered from these five coreholes are plotted on the logs except for the upper two at DD-1 projected from corehole CA-27. Bracketed values refer to analyses made on disseminated organic carbon whereas unbracketed ones are on carbonate material. The pattern of these results demonstrates problems involved with exact radiocarbon ages of events.

(1984) based on many anomalous results for the same range of age differences from the southern Levant, especially from Early Bronze sites of the Dead Sea region. He considered archaeological dating for ages younger than Early Bronze more precise than radiocarbon dating. This does not mean that such results from sites of older ages are necessarily more reliable nor does it mean that all radiocarbon results are erroneous.

In spite of their variations, a downward increase in radiocarbon dates and their agreement with the average rates of deposition are common. According to this criterion, ages of the two dates for disseminated organic carbon in samples 1 and 3 also can be accepted. Based on similar considerations it is rational to trust the two apparent sequential ages of samples 6 and 7 made on carbonate carbon. These four results as plotted on the logs of Figures 3.1 and 3.2 express only order of magnitude of ages and not precise values. Gilead (1993) applied a similar approach to improve radiocarbon dating reliability of Chalcolithic and Early Bronze sites in south Israel. He recommended the use of large numbers of radiocarbon analyses in series from the same sites, correlating the results with those from ancient Egypt having the same archaeological cultures and using new high precision techniques. The average results of the latter differ from uncalibrated ones by nearly 1,200 years.

The climatic fluctuation pattern for Holocene identified from gamma-ray logs of drill holes in the south basin agrees with that of intensities during wet subphases inferred from Mount Sedom caves; still the true age of Climatic Wet Phase III (Figures 3.1, 3.2), is problematic. According to radiocarbon analyses of tree twigs found in galleries of the caves, the peak of that phase should have been between 4580 ± 90 B.P. and 4250 ± 95 B.P.—between the end of Early Bronze II and the middle of the Intermediate Bronze age. Traditional archaeological chronology of Early Bronze sequences at the Bab edh-Dhr'a and Numeira sites, the Beth She'an basin, and Beth Yerah clearly indicates that this wet climatic phase occurred sometime after the end of the Intermediate Bronze age and ended with the Late Bronze between 3900 B.P. and 3200 B.P. A discrepancy of 600 and 1,000 years between apparent ages of this wet phase is inferred by comparing results of the geochronological-radiocarbon dating analyses made in studies along the Dead Sea–Jordan Valley at archaeological sites near the geological ones. Such a gap is too large to have been caused just by errors in radiocarbon analysis. An alternative is an earlier wet subphase of appreciably less intensity and shorter duration (200 to 400 years) sometime between 5000 B.P. and 4600 B.P. during Early Bronze I and II (Figure 3.2). This interpretation disagrees with radiocarbon ages of the Sedom cave driftwood. To avoid confusion, traditional archaeological chronology has been used as far as possible in correlation efforts, not necessarily because it should be considered correct but because it is more consistent and based upon a

broad spectrum of regional data as well as on a large number of radiocarbon analyses.

Stratigraphic Correlation between the South and North Basins

A 34.5-m corehole was made near the southwest corner of the Dead
Sea north basin near the shore (–394 m m.s.l.) at the delta of the Ze'elim
River (Yechieli et al., 1993, and personal communication). It was drilled
using the shell and auger method with no casing and no added mud or
water. The upper 24 m of the hole contained poorly sorted and unconsolidated detritus with two distinct gravel layers, each about 4 m thick.
The upper gravel layer is near the top of the hole; the other is at a depth
of 10 to 14 m. A few marl layers are interbedded within this unit but
only one at a depth of about 4 m is similar to Lisan facies—alternating
laminae of white aragonite and green-gray marl. A 6.5-m rocksalt layer
underlies the detrital unit between depths of 24 and 30.5 m. Farther
down is a 2.5-m-thick unlaminated green and gray clay layer containing disseminated small gypsum crystals and very large halite ones. The
lowest 1.5 m penetrated by that hole consists of alternating white aragonite and dark clay laminae that characterize most sediments of the
Lisan Formation. Some gypsum crystals also are at the top of that layer.

^{230}Th/^{234}U age analyses were made on two samples of Lisan-type
sediments from the drill hole. The upper one is actually from a nearby
outcrop equivalent to the marl layers 4 m beneath the top of the hole;
its age is less than 2000 B.P. The second sample is from a depth of 33.5 m,
1 m above the bottom of the hole; its age is 21,100 ± 1800 B.P. (Kaufman
et al., 1992). Six pieces of wood were selected from different depths of
the bailed samples and analyzed for radiocarbon dates. The uppermost
piece is from a depth of 16 m with an age of 8255 ± 70 B.P., two are
from 18 m with ages of 8385 ± 35 B.P. and 8390 ± 8 B.P., two from 22 m
or 2 m above the rocksalt layer with ages of 8405 ± 70 B.P. and 8440 ±
95 B.P., and the sixth piece from beneath the rocksalt at a depth of 32.5 m
with a radiocarbon age of 11,315 ± 80 B.P. (Yechieli et al., 1993, table
1). This sixth piece is from 1.5 m above the lowest Lisan-type layers,
the ^{230}Th/^{234}U age of which is 21,100 B.P. The age difference of nearly
10,000 years between the sixth radiocarbon result and the lower thorium analysis must represent an erosional gap. Accordingly it is assumed
that the rocksalt layer is younger than 11,315 ± 80 B.P. and older than
8440 ± 95 B.P., supporting the hypothesis of an extreme drop of the Dead
Sea level during its transition from Lisan Lake stage.

A gradual upward facies change was noted through the lowest
10.5 m (24 to 34.5 m depth). This implies a climatically induced transition toward increasing salinity of brine from which these sediments were
derived. It begins with a Lisan-type marl layer at the bottom, contin-

ues with green clays containing no carbonate but disseminated gypsum and halite crystals, and ends with a rocksalt layer at the top. This pattern reduces the likelihood of a nondepositional hiatus or erosional unconformity above the finely laminated Lisan Formation.

Considering the difference between the 21,100 B.P. thorium age of the underlying Lisan marl and the 11,315 B.P. radiocarbon age of the wood sample just above, the sample from the lowest depth analyzed could be out of place or caved in, as suggested for the other five samples. A nondepositional hiatus is more likely at the depth of 24 m, the contact between the rocksalt layer and overlying sandy marl. The 6.5-m rocksalt layer may correlate with the third-from-the-top layer at corehole CA-14 and DD-1 in the south basin (Figures 3.2, 3.5) or with climatic cycle 7 of the Würm glacial epoch. Possibly the depositional process of the rocksalt continued for a time within the trough of the north basin but already had ceased along its fringes, where the Ze'elim River auger hole is located, as well as within the south basin. As no indication for a rocksalt layer is evident on the gamma-ray log within the time span of about 14,000 to 8000 B.P. (climatic cycle 8 of the Würm or Climatic Wet Phase I of Holocene) the time of deposition of that layer may have been between 17,000 and 15,000 B.P.

Although the 34.5-m auger hole produced an imperfect record for the latest Pleistocene to Holocene sedimentary sequence, it is discussed here because it is the only available source of detailed drill hole stratigraphic information from the Dead Sea north basin for this time span. Care in interpretation allows the making of deductions about regional tectonic and climatic history for the general time within which the cities of Sodom, Gomorrah, and Jericho existed and perished.

Facies Distribution across Lisan Lake

Three sedimentary facies were contemporary in different parts of Lisan Lake (Begin et al., 1974). A detritus-rich diatomite facies is found in the north part within the Sea of Galilee and Beth She'an basins (Figure 1.2) and at the northwest fringe of the Dead Sea basin near the West border fault. It is within a structurally controlled small secondary basin that hangs at an elevation of –230 m m.s.l. or about 70 m above the –300 m m.s.l. paleobottom contour of Lisan Lake (Neev and Emery, 1967, fig. 15). An aragonite facies lies in the north-central segment of the basin at the Adam (Damiya) Bridge and south. A gypsum facies occurs between Jericho and Mezada. This threefold division delineates the southward increase in total amount of evaporation or increased concentration of dissolved ions as well as a decrease in detrital fraction supplied to the lake. These effects were produced by the southward increase of the regional thermal gradient and greater distance from the main inflow of fresh water into Lisan Lake. A fourth facies was later described by Begin, Nathan, and Ehrlich (1980) and Druckman et al. (1987) at the south end between Mount Sedom and Hazeva (Figures 1.2, 1.3). This facies is characterized by fine-grained quartz debris laminated with oolitic aragonite. It originated from the supply of fresh water coming into the lake from farther south because of high rainfall over the Negev and Edom mountains during Pleistocene pluvial stages.

Additional and more detailed studies have been conducted recently on diatomic facies (Ehrlich and Noel, 1988) in the north and the habitat, including temperature and salinity dependence of microalgae (Dor and Ehrlich, 1987; Dor and Paz, 1989). It was found that microalgae such as *Aphanothece halophytica* Fremy, which form hollow spherical aragonite-walled cells 10 to 15 microns in diameter, coexist with diatoms under similar optimal conditions, 16° to 48° C and 40 to 180 o/oo salinities. The diatoms of the Lisan Formation are dominated by *Nitzchia sigma* that form narrow and flat hairlike threads 300 to 400 microns long at about the same optimum temperature and salinity. Infralaminated papershale-like diatomites are deposited in the purest habitat with more indigenous biogenic and less detrital material. The mixed algal-diatom communities form gelatinous substrates on bottom sediments and develop mats within the shallow environment of littoral flats. Mats in Lisan Lake seasonally grew and trapped detrital material to form infralaminae upon their deaths but revived during the following season. Outcrops of bundles of these white and dark diatomites contain layers as thick as 30 cm that alternate with thicker, more detrital, and less clearly laminated layers.

Preservation of laminated structures within bottom sediments of Lisan Lake indicates the absence of burrowers. This has two possible explanations. Laminated sediments may have settled at the bottom of the Lower Water Mass that was devoid of free-oxygen-inhibiting burrowers; the weakness of this explanation is that these diatoms are benthic forms—restricted to very shallow water and to oxygenated environments. A better explanation may be the peculiar ionic composition of the Dead Sea–Lisan Lake brines. Ehrlich and Noel (1988) considered the very high Mg/Ca ratio as inhibiting animal life other than some unicellular types of algae, cyanobacteria, and bacteria that live within bottom sediments of both euxinic (devoid of free oxygen) and aerated parts of the water column. M. Ginzburg (1982) concluded that survival of at least two types of micro-organisms in Dead Sea brine depends on specific ability to limit quantities of sodium ions that can enter their cells. Considering the unique combination of environmental conditions required for existence, the diatom and microalgal mats may serve as sensitive indicators for changes in depth, temperature, and salinity of Lisan Lake. Variations in their distribution patterns may indicate changes in ancient climates.

Chronology of Climatic Phases of Late Pleistocene

Although the psychological impact of tectonic events such as those of the Sodom, Gomorrah, and Jericho sagas was greater than the gradual climatic changes, the latter seem an efficient tool to establish a useful chronology. This is especially true for the Dead Sea area where changes of climate have left prominent imprints on the sequence of alternating sedimentary layers deposited from brines, diluted brines, or fresh waters. Tectonic events with or without volcanism have been incorporated. Discussion of climatic chronology is separated for Late Pleistocene and Holocene because abundant archaeological remains yield much greater knowledge of changes in Holocene climates. Climatic phases of Late Pleistocene are marked by Arabic numbers 1 to 8; those of Holocene are identified by Roman numbers I to IV (Figures 3.1, 3.2).

New absolute dates (^{230}Th/^{234}U method) of the Samra and Lisan formations in the Dead Sea region (Kaufman et al., 1992) corroborate earlier results by Kaufman (1971). They indicate ranges of about 350,000 to 110,000 B.P. for the Samra Formation and 60,000 to 18,000 or 15,000 B.P. for the Lisan Formation. Analyses were made on 30 samples from eight columnar sections scattered on land from north of the sea at Beth Ha'arava southwest to Hazeva, a distance of 110 km. The dates reflect an erosional unconformity between the two formations whose length decreases from the south and west fringes of the two lakes toward their central parts. At the south a time gap of more than 300,000 years was detected across less than 10 m of the relevant columnar sections; farther north this gap is only 30,000 years. Large hiatuses also were found within the Samra Formation where a 125,300-year span, from 240,900 to 115,600 B.P., was identified across a section less than 5-m thick where no lithologic difference was recognized. Other physically unrecognizable unconformities probably exist within these two formations. Rock-salt layers, sodium-rich and possibly potassium-rich, may have been deposited in deeper parts of Samra and Lisan lakes during shrinking stages when their areal dimensions were about the same as those of the Dead Sea.

The long time span of about 300,000 years related by Kaufman et al. (1992) for the Samra Formation corresponds with three long climatic cycles of global magnitude, as indicated by variations of heavy oxygen isotopes in calcareous tests of pelagic (swimming or floating) foraminiferans within ocean floor sediments (Table 3.2). Only future deep coreholes within the troughs of the south and north basins may provide information about the natures and ages of rock units deposited during that time span.

Interpretation of gamma-ray logs, lithologic logs, and radiocarbon dates of the CA-14, DD-1 (25 m deep) corehole and the 80-m-deep hole (Figures 2.10, 3.1, 3.2, 3.5) leads to a conclusion that the uppermost

Table 3.2 Late Pleistocene Climatic Stages—
Global and Dead Sea Distributions

Global stage*	Formations (Dead Sea region)	European equivalent	Age (10^3 B.P.)*	$\partial^{18}O$ (extreme values)*	Type of climate
1	Dead Sea	Holocene	12–0	−2.0	Interglacial
2–4	Lisan	Würm	70–12	+1.8	Glacial
5	Lisan-Samra	Riss-Würm	128–70	−2.1	Interglacial
6	Samra	Riss	183–128	+1.6	Glacial
7	?	?	240–183	−1.8	Interglacial
8	?	?	270–240	+1.0	Glacial
9	?	?	330–270	−2.0	Interglacial
10	?	?	360–330	+1.0	Glacial

*After Imbrie et al. (1984, table 6 and figs. 7, 8).

section from −410 m m.s.l. to the surface was deposited during most of the Holocene from about 8000 B.P. to the present. Underlying sediments between −450 m and about −410 m m.s.l. accumulated as the Lisan Formation during the Würm glacial stage from about 70,000 to 11,000 B.P. The lithology of these formations consists of Lisan-type marls from diluted brines and rocksalts from concentrated brines. Marls dominate throughout the Lisan Formation; rocksalts are more abundant in the Holocene Dead Sea Formation. The lower 30 m of the 80-m hole (Figure 3.1) is chiefly rocksalt layers that may continue even deeper. This long dry period probably is equivalent to the Riss-Würm Interglacial existing between 128,000 and 70,000 B.P. (Table 3.3; Charlesworth, 1957; Horowitz, 1979, table 5.2).

An important observation regarding the Würm pluvial stage is that seven or eight relatively thick rocksalt layers are interbedded within the Lisan marl sequence. This implies that levels of Lisan Lake dropped seven or eight times during the Würm glacial stage to at least as low as −400 m m.s.l. with intervening levels as high as −180 m m.s.l. Thus seven or eight cycles of very dry climate occurred during the Würm. The duration of the last low level of the Lisan Formation (marked as cycle 7 in Figures 3.1, 3.2) is estimated as 2,000 years between 17,000 and 15,000 B.P. based on its 3-m thickness and on radiocarbon dates above and below it. This dry substage may be correlated with most of the Kebaran age of the Epipaleolithic when Lisan Lake shrank (Bar-Yosef, 1987).

The last four climatic cycles of Lisan Lake occurred between 25,000 and 10,000 B.P. (cycles 5, 6, 7, 8 in Figure 3.2). At least four different pluvial peaks appear on the gamma-ray log during the same time span. This sequence is implied from the results of radiocarbon analyses made on the carbonate fraction of sediments collected from elevated terraces at the south and southwest periphery near the highest level reached by Lisan Lake. Elevations and ages are as follows: −180 m m.s.l. 24,000

± 900 B.P. (Neev and Emery, 1967); –209 m 21,350 ± 700 B.P. (L736-D; D. Thurber, Lamont Geol. Obs., 1967, personal communication to Neev); –200 m 20,400 ± 400 B.P., –190 m 14,600 ± 240 B.P. (Druckman, Margaritz, and Sneh, 1987).

Changes in level of Lisan Lake recorded by Late Pleistocene sediments show that fluctuating levels of the Dead Sea were part of a similar long series produced by variations in climate. Thus the changes in level and their climatic causes during the time of Sodom and Gomorrah are not to be considered unusual or abnormal for the region.

Chronology of Climatic Phases of Holocene

Phase I: Transition from Pleistocene

The last pluvial or cold phase within the Würm glacial stage perhaps corresponds with the Geometric Kebaran, Natufian, and Pre-Pottery Neolithic B ages (Table 3.3). It began about 15,000 B.P., peaked 13,000 to 12,000 B.P., and ended about 7800 B.P.—a time span of 7,200 years. This is supported by the relatively great thickness (3 to 5 m) of a marl bed that represents Climatic Wet Phase I according to lithologic and gamma-ray logs of coreholes CA-14 and DD-1 and wide distribution of this bed across the Dead Sea south basin as well as from results of eight radiocarbon age analyses (Tables 3.1, 3.3; Figures 3.1, 3.2, 3.5). More precise identification of the timing of different climatic changes within Phase I was reached by correlating geological results with cultural changes shown by studies in other disciplines. The comprehensive regional prehistoric investigations by Bar-Yosef and Mintz (1979) and Bar-Yosef (1987) produced a clear picture of changing demographic cultural patterns. Changes of pollen spectra as studied by A. Horowitz (1979, 1992) also helped.

In Figure 3.1 and Table 3.3 Climatic Wet Phase I of Holocene overlaps cycle 8 of Pleistocene. Its long time span from 15,000 to 7800 B.P. indicates that the last major cold phase of the Würm glaciation stage started in Late Pleistocene and declined within Early Holocene. It consisted of several climatic fluctuations or subphases somewhat subdued on gamma-ray logs, perhaps because of abruptness in the changes. The last cold phase of the Würm was preceded by an extreme dry phase between 17,000 and 15,000 B.P. (cycle 7 on Figure 3.2) correlated with the Kebaran age. This probably is a valid observation based on the presence of a deep low on the gamma-ray curves of coreholes DD-1 to DD-5 corresponding with a 2-m massive rocksalt layer on the lithologic log of the CA-14 corehole. The evidence does not agree with relatively high content of arboreal pollen found by Horowitz in sediments within Kebaran sites, 5–12% as compared with the 1–2% at the present. Such contrast of opinion could be explained if the time span of the Kebaran were really 19,000 to 14,500 B.P. as suggested by A. Horowitz (1992,

Table 3.3 Chronology of Climatic Phases and Wet Subphases in the Dead Sea Region during the Past 24,000 Years (including High Dead Sea Levels)

| Geological periods and archaeological cultures | Climatic | | | Duration (years) | Dead Sea levels (m m.s.l) |
	Phase intervals B.P.	Wet interim subphases	B.P.		
Late Holocene	IV 3200–0			3200	−300 to 400
		d	162–17	145	−390
		c	810–750	60	−385
		b	1800–1500	400	−375
		a	2700–2300	400	−375
Mid-Holocene (Middle to Late Bronze)	III 3900–3200			700	−300 to −350
		b	3500–3200	300	
		a	3900–3600	300	
Mid-Holocene (Late Neolithic to Early Bronze– Intermediate Bronze)	II 7800–3900			3900	−350 to −400
		b	4900–4650	250	−350
		a	6350–6000	350	−400
Early Holocene (Natufian to Pre-Pottery Neolithic B)	I 12,500–7800			4700	−190 to −300
		a	9000–7800	500	−200
Late Pleistocene Epipaleolithic (Geometric Kebaran)	(8) 15,000–12,500			2500	−180 to −250
Late Pleistocene Epipaleolithic (Kebaran)	(7) 17,000(?)–15,000			2000	−300 to −400
Late Pleistocene Upper Paleolithic	(6) 40,000–19,000			21,000	−180 to −400

p. 417). Pollen content in Kebaran sediments may represent an average of data from deposits accumulated at the same sites from previous cold conditions of climatic cycle 6 (20,000 to 17,000 B.P.) and dry warm conditions of cycle 7 that followed (17,000 to 15,000 B.P.; Figures 3.1, 3.2).

Cold wet conditions inferred by A. Horowitz (1992) for the Geometric Kebaran Age is supported by Figure 3.2. Overall warming and drying climatic processes beyond its peak (13,000 to 12,000 B.P.) can be related to the Natufian and Pre-Pottery Neolithic A ages, as supported by results of studies in sedimentology, archaeology, and palynology. Low arboreal pollen content (2–4%) is found in Late Natufian with even lower values to 0% during the short transition between Natufian and Pre-Pottery Neolithic. Unusually high contents (10–20%) characterize the Pre-Pottery Neolithic B age. These changes are expected to have left stronger expressions on the gamma-ray log but, for a yet unknown reason, they are hard to identify exactly on this fluctuating segment of the graph.

Unlike in earlier work (Neev and Emery, 1967; Neev, 1978) no evidence was found in the present study for a major desiccation event during transition between Pleistocene and Holocene, about 12,000 to 11,000 B.P. Mildly warmer climate could have started during the break between the Natufian and Pre-Pottery Neolithic ages 11,000 years ago or even somewhat earlier. After an initial recession of Lisan Lake at this time, extensive swamps and small lakes were left within its depositional plain. Climatic Wet Subphase I-a (Table 3.3) occurred sometime between 9000 and 7800 B.P., or during Pre-Pottery Neolithic B age. Although indicated by pollen analyses and corroborated by extensive distribution of swamp sediments at the Kinneret Plain, Beth She'an basin, and Jericho, this wet phase is not well pronounced on the gamma-ray curve (Figure 3.2). Perhaps it was suppressed by the overall declining curve that followed the 12,500 B.P. peak of the last major climatic wet (cold) phase of the Pleistocene.

During the wet climatic interval of Pre-Pottery Neolithic B (PPNB), the Jordan River gorge was gradually eroding through sills that dammed both the Sea of Galilee and Beth She'an basin on their south sides. By then, 7800 B.P. or the beginning of Pottery Neolithic, Climatic Phase II was initiated. During the transition from Boreal to Climatic Optimum or Atlantic Interval (Gary, McAfee, and Wolf, 1974; Bar-Yosef, 1987), Lisan Lake shrank drastically. During the dry climatic subphase of the Pottery Neolithic and Early Chalcolithic ages, the Dead Sea could have reached even below –400 m m.s.l.

Radiocarbon age of a wood fragment from the highest 5-m wide cave in Mount Sedom implied to Frumkin et al. (1991) that a relatively wet climatic phase caused a high sea level (–315 m m.s.l.) about 7,100 years ago. This dating may be incorrect because of radiocarbon problems as suggested by data from the south basin, which indicates that by this time the shrinking water body had fallen nearly to the critical low level of –400 m m.s.l. and rocksalt had begun to precipitate.

Phase II: Climatic Optimum—Mostly Dry

Climatic Optimum and Atlantic Interval are synonymous, defining the driest as well as the warmest postglacial climatic period between about 7,500 to 4,500 years ago (Gary et al., 1974, p. 45). Neev and Emery (1967, fig. 17; p. 28) interpreted the 3-to-8-m-thick second rocksalt layer from the middle-lower part of the Dead Sea Formation in the south basin

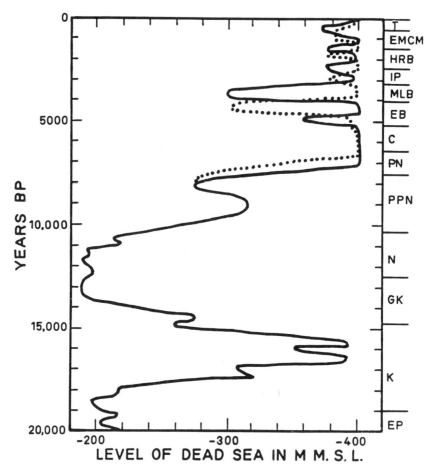

Figure 3.6. Interpreted climatic fluctuation patterns in the Dead Sea region during the past 20,000 years. Vertical scale on left is in years before present, as compared with depths given in Figures 3.1, 3.2, and 3.5. Horizontal scale represents the changing levels below mean sea (ocean) level. Continuous line is based on coreholes in south basin, whereas dotted line for the past 8,000 years is from Frumkin et al. (1991, fig. 8) for the Mount Sedom caves. The two lines are similar with a few hundred years discrepancy attributed to interpretations of radiocarbon dates. Vertical scale on right denotes sequence of ages: EP = Epipaleolithic; K = Kebaran; GK = Geometric Kebaran; N = Natufian; PPN = Pre-Pottery Neolithic; PN = Pottery (Ceramic) Neolithic; C = Chalcolithic; EB = Early Bronze; MLB = Middle and Late Bronze; IP = Israel and Persian; HRB = Hellenic and Roman + Byzantine; EMCM = Early Moslem, Crusader, and Mamaluk; T = Turkish.

as representing the driest period during Holocene—between 6500 and 5500 B.P. New data indicate this generally corresponds with Climatic Dry Phase II, which began about 7800 B.P. and ended about 3900 B.P. It existed during the Pottery Neolithic, Chalcolithic, and Early Bronze archaeological ages (Table 3.3; Figures 3.1, 3.2, 3.6) but was interrupted by two wet subphases 350 and 250 years long (II-a and II-b).

There is little doubt that both wet subphases did occur. The first one, Climatic Subphase II-a, corresponds with Early to Middle Chalcolithic (Ghassulian) ages, which peaked throughout Canaan during the last third of the 4th millennium B.C. (Kenyon, 1979, p. 64), equivalent to a calibrated radiocarbon time of 6300 to 6000 B.P. (Gilead, 1993). The settling of large prosperous farming communities that survived for several hundred years in south Israel, mostly at Beersheva Valley and Teleilat Ghassul, suggests that the climatic regime then was wetter than at present. The site of Teleilat Ghassul is about 15 km southeast of Jericho east of the Jordan River on barren land quite remote from a perennial water supply. That agricultural community lived prosperously on dry farming and grazing in an area that now cannot support farms except with irrigation. A climatic change is inferred to have occurred during the Ghassulian age from dry conditions that characterized the average of Climatic Dry Phase II to wetter times. That their advanced culture compared with the primitive one of Pottery Neolithic inhabitants of Jericho suggests that Ghassulians were newcomers who had immigrated to Canaan. Results of studies made by Bar-Yosef and Mintz (1979), Gophna (1979), A. Horowitz (1979, 1992), and Gilead (1993) laid out the distribution pattern of Ghassulian-Chalcolithic seminomadic settlements all over Canaan during the 7th to 6th millennium B.P. By then the Beersheva-Arad Valley and northwest Negev were occupied by about 100,000 people in 200 sites (David Allon, a regional archaeologist, personal communication).

Three of four radiocarbon dates from the "Treasures Cave" at Nahal Mishmar between En Gedi and Mezada where a collection of sophisticated copper alloy tools was found are from the second quarter of the 6th millennium B.P. (Gilead, 1993). "The Ghassulians, like the Jews of the 2nd century A.D., may have taken refuge in barren and almost inaccessible spots in the face of an approaching enemy" (Kenyon, 1979, pp. 62–64), but this enemy did not inherit and settle the deserted lands of the Ghassulians. The hiatus found everywhere in Canaan between Ghassulian and Early Bronze settlements suggests a return to the dry climate that characterized Climatic Dry Phase II.

Wet Subphase II-b lasted between 4900 and 4650 B.P. as indicated by the settling, flourishing, and sudden decay and desertion of the city of Arad (Figures 1.2, 1.3) during Early Bronze I and II. This prosperous city in which no facilities to store water have been found is at the fringe of the present desert nearly halfway between Beersheva and the Dead

Sea. It is suggested that climatic conditions during part of Early Bronze were appreciably wetter than at present. Abandonment of Arad probably is associated with a desertification process that gradually developed toward the Intermediate Bronze age (Gophna, 1979; R. Amiran, 1986; D. Amiran, 1991).

Plant twigs sampled from Mount Sedom caves (Frumkin et al., 1991) are significant indicators of climatic conditions. Four samples were identified as oak *Quercus calliprinos* (Webb) whose radiocarbon ages span a short time, 4600 to 4200 B.P. Their average age is supported by a 4410 ± 320 B.P. radiocarbon age of disseminated organic carbon extracted from a layer of Lisan facies marl several meters thick in corehole CA-27 (Neev and Emery, 1967, p. 28). This layer probably correlates with a 2-m layer of similar lithology between depths of –405 and –407 m m.s.l. in coreholes DD-1 and CA-14 interbedded between two salt beds (Figures 3.2, 3.5). The four oak twig samples came from only three caves whose outlets at relatively high elevations denote a brief wet period in which oaks could flourish. The rest of the samples were from different caves and elevations with ages both older and younger, all representing flora of dry desert communities. It is inferred that these twigs from Mount Sedom are too young to reflect Climatic Wet Subphases II-a or II-b and could represent a younger phase or subphase of extreme wet cold climate.

Only one pronounced peak of high radiation indicating a wet subphase is superimposed on the segment of gamma-ray values in the log of the DD-1 corehole representing Climatic Phase II (Figures 3.1, 3.2, 3.5). Its position on the curve shows that this short but unique and well-pronounced peak of 50 API units should be correlated with Climatic Wet Subphase II-b. It is not yet understood why gamma radiation for Wet Subphase II-a is so subdued because Ghassulian cultural indications for wet conditions as well as sedimentological ones from Beth She'an basin are firm. A possible explanation could involve a change in the annual distribution pattern of precipitation, such as summer rains during Early Chalcolithic age that did not necessarily cause an appreciable increase of average yearly rainfall.

A northward shift of the monsoonal rain system within the Asiatic-African atmospheric belt probably occurred during times of global warming conditions (Klein et al., 1970). In extreme cases the northernmost fringes of that system might have affected the southernmost Levant (Goldberg and Rosen, 1987, p. 29). The resultant climatic pattern could have created environmental conditions necessary for extensive grazing in the loess areas of the Negev Desert. It could also have caused sufficient wetness in the rugged mountains of Sinai, the Negev, and Judea to enable moderate growth of oak and olive trees. If during Ghassulian or Middle Chalcolithic ages (Fiure 3.2) the overall yearly ratios of runoff to evaporation in the Dead Sea rift had not increased above the average during Climatic Dry Phase II, the process of rocksalt precipitation may have continued and Lisan-type marls would not have been deposited.

A most pronounced archaeological break occurred by the end of Early Bronze III age (Figure 3.2), about 4350 B.P. or 450 years before the beginning of Climatic Wet Phase III. It continued until the end of Intermediate Bronze, synonymous with both Early Bronze IV and Middle Bronze I. The cultural-demographic changes probably resulted from the combined effects of severe tectonic activity near the end of Early Bronze III and gradual drying that followed. These changes are indicated by a shift from large communities with a mixed urban and agricultural life-style into dwindling semi-nomadic settlements based mostly on grazing (Gophna, 1992). This conclusion is emphasized by changed siting of important urban centers along the Jordan–Dead Sea rift as well as all over Canaan during the end of Early Bronze III age.

Processes of destruction and desertion not caused by conquests also occurred along the coastal areas of Syria and Lebanon; inner regions of Syria and Jordan east of the Jordan River were less affected (Gophna, 1992). Such a relationship of selective destruction in different areas can best be explained by the pattern of seismic tectonic activity. This is similar to one inferred from historical data of the Mideast during the first 17 centuries A.D. as studied by Ambraseys (1978, p. 202, fig.1). The largest historical earthquakes in that region occurred along the border between West and East Anatolia that extended south along northwest Syria, Lebanon, and Israel (Figures 1.1, 1.2, 2.18). Seismicity alternated between Anatolia from Longitude 35°E to 40°E and farther south with very long periods of relative inactivity (Ambraseys, 1971). Such a pattern can imply that both the Arabian and Sinai plates as well as the East Mediterranean plate are moving north separately at different rates.

The last part of Climatic Phase II occurred during Intermediate Bronze age between 4350 and 3900 B.P., although all of it could be defined as a dry subphase. Aridity became extreme between 4200 and 3900 B.P. so the population that had dwindled during the period of intense tectonic activity diminished further and large territories of the entire region became deserted (Gophna, 1992; Weiss et al., 1993).

Phase III: Mostly Wet

A dramatic change into Climatic Wet Phase III followed Intermediate Bronze age (Tables 3.3, 3.4; Figure 3.2). Probably these wetter conditions lasted about 700 years between 3900 and 3200 B.P., from the beginning of Middle Bronze II until after the transition from Late Bronze into Iron age in a succession of three or four subphases. Volcanic eruptions such as the Santorini-Thera event 1627–1623 B.C. (Zielinski et al., 1994) could have caused some of these wet climatic conditions.

Table 3.4   Holocene Cultural Ages in Israel

Ages		Dates (B.P.)	Dates (calendar)
Turkish to 20th Century	*	500–70	1918–1517
Mamlukian		700–500	1517–1270
Crusader	*	900–700	1291–1092
Early Moslem to Crusader		1360–900	1092–640
Byzantine to Early Moslem	*	1700–1360	640–300
Hellenistic to Late Roman		2330–1700	300 A.D.–300 B.C.
Late Iron	*	2700–2330	300–700
Early Iron		3200–2700	700–1200
Late Bronze to Early Iron	*	3500–3200	1200–1500
Middle Bronze to Late Bronze	*	3900–3500	1500–1900
Intermediate Bronze		4350–3900	1900–2350
Early Bronze (EB I, II, III)	*	5300–4350	2350–3300
Chalcolithic to Earliest Bronze	*	6500–5300	3300–4500
Late Neolithic		7800–6500	4500–5800
Early Neolithic (PPNB)	*	10,300–7800	5800–8300
Natufian (Mesolithic)	*	12,500–10,300	8300–10,500
Geometric Kebaran	*	15,000–12,500	10,500–13,000
Kebaran		17,000–15,000	13,000–15,000
Epipaleolithic (lower part)	*	22,000–17,000	15,000–20,000
Late Pleistocene (Late Paleolithic)		30,000–22,000?	20,000–28,000

*Cultural breaks associated with wet climatic phases.

Physical evidences for Climatic Wet Phase III were found in the Dead Sea region, south basin, Mount Sedom, Jericho, Beth Yerah or the Sea of Galilee, Beth She'an basin, Uvda Valley (southeast Negev), Khirbet el Umbashi in the Bashan volcanic field of Jebel Druze in southern Syria (Fig. 1.2), and north Mesopotamia (Weiss et al., 1993). Traditional archaeological chronology of Early Bronze age in Israel and Jordan indicates that both Beth Yerah and Bab edh-Dhr'a were inhabited between Early Bronze I and Intermediate Bronze (Early Bronze IV) between about 5000 and 4200 B.P. Although Frumkin et al. (1991) correlated most of the time span of Climatic Wet Phase III with Early Bronze III (4600 to 4200 B.P.), it is possible that this wet phase occurred during Middle to Late Bronze or 3900 to 3200 B.P. If this interpretation is correct, Climatic Wet Phase III should be younger by 500 to 1,000 years than relevant radiocarbon ages of Mount Sedom caves, or between 4600 and 4200 B.P.

The dilemma is difficult to solve because radiocarbon dates of wet phase sediments in nonarchaeological sites are being confronted by younger archaeological ages of human-occupied layers overlain by sediments deposited during the same wet phase. The 700-year duration of this phase is confirmed by information about the rate of deposition and thickness of the relevant marl layer in the Dead Sea south basin.

Information regarding wet climate only since the Middle Bronze II age comes from reliable stratigraphic data, both archaeological and sedimentological. Its correctness is attested by other considerations, such as extensive settling during Middle to Late Bronze, between 3900 and 3200 B.P., of new human societies with highly developed cultural skills in urban fortified cities, and of affluent agrarian societies in the northwest Negev region as well as by their intensive regional commercial ties (Kochavi, 1967; Gophna, 1979; David Allon, personal communication).

Phase IV: Mostly Dry

Climatic Phase IV extended from 3200 B.P. to the present (Tables 3.3, 3.4). It contains four short wet intervals of 60 to 400 years separated by longer times of relatively dry climate. These are indicated by both gamma-ray logs of coreholes in the south basin and high levels inferred from the Mount Sedom caves. During both Climatic Wet Subphases IV-a and IV-b, the sea rose to an elevation of −375 m m.s.l., 2700 to 2300 B.P. and 1100 to 700 B.P., respectively, according to radiocarbon ages of wood fragments found within the galleries. Climatic Wet Subphases IV-c and IV-d are not recognized as separate and prominent positive peaks on the gamma-ray log though they were traced as independent galleries in Mount Sedom caves at elevations of −385 and −390 m m.s.l., respectively.

The duration of Climatic Wet Subphase IV-c could have been appreciably shorter than the 400 years inferred from a dendrochronological study by Waisel and Liphschitz (1968, as quoted by Klein, 1986, chrono sheet no. 4). Tree-ring counts and thicknesses of *Juniperus phoenica* that began to grow in the nearby Negev mountains about 880 years ago indicate that the wet climatic episode lasted only 60 years between 810 and 750 B.P. Climatic Wet Interval IV-d extended between A.D. 1830 and 1975; its peak of about −390 m m.s.l. in the Dead Sea occurred between A.D. 1896 and 1932.

False Indications of High Levels of the Dead Sea

There have been several published suggestions about high levels of the Dead Sea during Roman and post-Roman times (Klein, 1986; Issar, Tsoar, and Levin, 1989). The observations on which they are based may have simpler explanations not involving such recent high levels.

The inner wall of the Assembly Hall at the Essene settlement at Khirbet Qumran at the northwest corner of the Dead Sea with an elevation of −325 m m.s.l. was photographed in 1951 by de Vaux (1973). In that photograph a rather uniform horizontal strip of whitish cement about a half-meter wide plasters the upper part of the wall. By 1981, when photographed again by Klein (1986, p. 81, photos no. 30, 31, chrono sheet no. 2), only relict patches of that strip remained. The cement was analyzed by the late Dr. E. Gavish, who found it to be 80% aragonite and 20% calcite. Klein inferred that this crust had been precipitated from brines when the sea rose by 70 m to –330 m m.s.l. during the 145-year climatic cycle between 105 B.C. and A.D. 40. Examination of the 1951 photograph and the site by Neev revealed that the horizontal strip of crust was more like remains of artificial wall plaster than a water-sediment deposit. It appears to terminate upward sharply along a line about 20 cm beneath the top of the wall, parallel to the latter. The central segment of the wall steps down to the east about 30 cm as if the uppermost row of building stones had been omitted. The cement strip below it imitates that step exactly and extends even farther east parallel to the top. If the crust were a natural deposit from Dead Sea brine, such a stepping down would have been impossible. The mere presence of such crusts on building stones as much as 70 m above the present level should not be regarded as unequivocal evidence of deposition indicative of cover by brine.

During archaeological excavations in the Qumran ruins of 1957 to 1965, de Vaux (1973) also described adjacent caves numbered 4 and 5 and their contents. Klein (1986, pp. 86–88, chrono sheet no. 8) commented that the sea transgressed again between the years A.D. 930 and 1120, when its level reached –350 m m.s.l. and brines penetrated cave 4 but not cave 5. Abundant fragmented Dead Sea scrolls were found by de Vaux (1973, p. 100) in caves 4 and 5 that were dug into deltaic topset beds on which the Essene settlement of Qumran was built. The caves (Figure 3.7) are at elevations of about –350 and –340 m m.s.l. near the Qumran ruins. Fragments of scrolls were found scattered within the marl layer that fills cave 4 down to its original floor whereas "the fragments from cave 5 were lying under more than one meter of natural deposit."

No detailed sedimentological studies have been made of detrital marl and gravel deposits that filled caves 4 and 5. Following de Vaux's description of the sedimentary fill, Klein (1986) considered them to be *in situ* aquatic deposits from Dead Sea brines. It is more likely that the detrital marl was produced simply by disintegration and weathering of unconsolidated deltaic deposits that fell from ceilings and walls of the man-made caves onto their floors.

The site of Qumran was occupied by the Essenes for less than 200 years between about 100 B.C. and the destruction of the Second Temple in Jerusalem by the Romans in A.D. 68. This occupation was interrupted by one relatively short period between 31 and 8–9 B.C. either because of damage by a severe earthquake (Allegro, 1958, fig. 25; Figure 3.8) and fire (de Vaux, 1973, as cited by Klein, 1986, pp. 80, 81) or by Parthian conquest (Mazar et al., 1966). De Vaux considered that scrolls in the caves were torn and mutilated by Roman soldiers about A.D. 68 before they were covered by accumulated marl debris. Additionally it

Figure 3.7. Eroded delta of Lisan Lake at Wadi Qumran near northwest corner of the Dead Sea. Into these unconsolidated sediments were dug the caves in which the Qumran scrolls were hidden before the site was captured in A.D. 68 by Romans (Allegro, 1958). Photographed in 1969.

Figure 3.8. Staircase at Qumran faulted in 31 B.C. Photographed in 1969.

is well known that Bedouin of local tribes, motivated by antiquity traders from Bethlehem and Hebron, thoroughly, although not professionally, excavated most of the caves in the Judean Desert for pillaging and selling scrolls (Yadin, 1971, pp. 28–66).

Desertion and destruction of Tel Goren at En Gedi occurred simultaneously with the brief abandonment at Qumran but are related by Mazar, Dothan, and Dunayevsky (1966) to the Parthian raid some time between 40 and 37 B.C. Existence of that raid is indicated by ashes from fires and the collapse of buildings in the tel whose top is at –335 m m.s.l. No sedimentological indications were found at Tel Goren to corroborate submergence during that time.

A rodent midden at an elevation of –280 m m.s.l. was found in the northwest corner of the north basin near the Essene settlement at Qumran (Goodfriend, Magaritz, and Carmi, 1986). It included shells of land snails having a radiocarbon age of 6660 ± 400 B.P. The midden was preserved beneath a large block of dense reefoid dolomite slumped from the border fault escarpment over the deltaic sediments of Lisan Lake and was encrusted by a rocksalt deposit that they proposed had been formed from brine splashed from the sea when the level was high. This evidence cannot be accepted because the snail shell date corresponds with the age of the early part of Climatic Phase II when a rocksalt layer, 3–8 m thick, was precipitating from brines in the south basin (Figure 3.2). Consequently the level of that time (Climatic Optimum) must have been as low as –400 m m.s.l.

A third find quoted by Klein (1986) indicating a high elevation of the Dead Sea is a small rocksalt deposit described by Lynch (1849) from a Byzantine burial cave of about 1400 B.P. located within deltaic sediments just north of En Gedi at an elevation of –350 m m.s.l. This rocksalt is similar to one described by Goodfriend et al. (1986).

If the levels of the Dead Sea had reached –350 and –330 m m.s.l., respectively, during Early Roman and Crusader times, the scale of physical and cultural damage to the region would have been enormous and disastrous for inhabitants. Most settlements and their irrigated lands and installations around the south basin, such as Mazra'a and Es-Safi on the east, En Boqeq and En Gedi on the west, and others near the foot of Amazyahu fault escarpment in the south would have been submerged. Flooded areas would have included the fertile and precious date and balsam plantations of international fame at En Gedi, as well as the spas of Callirhoe (Zerka Main) and En Boqeq. Rise of sea level would have blocked the route between Judea and Moab across Lynch Strait east over the Lisan Peninsula. Except for one small island at its center, the peninsula would have been too deeply submerged to allow travel on foot.

In light of expected effects of damage from such flooding, it is even more surprising that skilled geographers and historians such as Pliny, Strabo, and Josephus, who lived during Early Roman times in nearby areas and included in their books many aspects of the Dead Sea, did not even mention it.

Crusaders used Roman roads leading from the Mediterranean coastal plain and Jerusalem to Moab and Arabia. They passed through the ford at Lynch Strait and the roads across the Lisan Peninsula up to Karak, the fortress of Moab, implied from the description of a Crusader raid into Arabia via Hebron in A.D. 1100 as written by Fulcher, a priest of Chartres who accompanied Boulogne on that raid and was quoted by Lamb (1953). Fulcher praised the fertility of the Sodom Plain and did not mention any such catastrophic event that would have occurred in his lifetime or earlier.

Analysts of climatic conditions in the Alps and the Black Sea region have assumed higher than present average temperatures there during the Early Roman period, 200 B.C. to A.D. 100 (Neumann, 1991, 1992). Such a warm climate does not agree with a cold climatic wet phase as implied by a level of −330 m m.s.l. in the Dead Sea.

4

Environmental Data for Specific Sites within the Dead Sea Region

Numeira, Bab edh-Dhr'a, and the Uvda Valley

Discussion of Early Bronze cultural history at Bab edh-Dhr'a and Numeira sites east of the Lisan Peninsula and on the northeast flank of the Dead Sea south basin is guided mostly by Rast (1987) and Rast and Schaub (1974, 1978, 1980, and 1981). This epoch was divided by Rast and Schaub into two sections according to traditional archaeological chronology. The first section is the urban period of Bab edh-Dhr'a (4890 to 4340 B.P.) including Early Bronze I, II, and III. The second is the posturban period (4340 to 4190 B.P.), Early Bronze IV or the Intermediate Bronze age according to Kochavi (1967), Kenyon (1979), Gophna (1992), and R. Amiran and Kochavi (1985) as well as Middle Bronze I according to Albright (1962). Although no prominent cultural hiatus separates these two sections, the transition between them contains abundant indications of extensive destruction and fire events brought about by natural disasters such as earthquakes. Donahue (1980, 1981) considered that not just one but two severe earthquakes occurred, one about 4400 B.P. and the other 4350 B.P. Numeira was totally and finally abandoned after the second earthquake, whereas Bab edh-Dhr'a was reinhabited apparently as a result of conquest by seminomadic people of the same cultural background. This second earthquake probably was the one by which Sodom and Gomorrah were totally destroyed.

Abrupt cultural changes also were recorded in the southeast Negev at Uvda Valley (Figure 1.2) during transition from Early Bronze III to

Middle Bronze I about 4300 B.P. These changes were from a gradually increasing population within a walled city having a life-style based on a combination of agriculture and animal husbandry into a more nomadic community with unfortified houses and primarily a grazing economy. According to Avner (1990, p. 133) "Subsequent to a brief climatic crisis at the end of the third millennium BC the climate improved, allowing the new culture to blossom in the desert." This climatic crisis could have been extreme dryness.

By the middle of the Intermediate Bronze age at about 4200 B.P., Bab edh-Dhr'a, the last Early Bronze site to survive was totally abandoned and the Dead Sea south basin remained basically unsettled for more than 1,500 years until Hellenistic time. That area was mentioned several times in the Bible only as an Iron age battlefield or as a route for armies (2 Samuel 8:13–14 and 2 Kings 14:7). No signs of another conquest or other human destruction have been identified to explain such desertion. The first 1,000 years could be explained by combined effects of an extremely dry climate during the latter part of the Intermediate Bronze and an extremely wet Climatic Phase III of the Middle and Late Bronze ages that followed. A rise of the sea level by nearly 100 m to about −300 m m.s.l., the highest reached during Holocene (Frumkin et al., 1991, fig. 3, climatic stage 3), would have flooded most agricultural soils of that basin. During this wet phase most of the Lisan Peninsula and most of the basin as far south as the foot of Amazyahu fault escarpment (Figure 1.4) were flooded by brines.

A paleobotanical study was made of natural flora, mostly grain and seeds, preserved in sediments of all occupied layers during Early Bronze I to Early Bronze IV at Bab edh-Dhr'a (4890 to 4190 B.P.) as well as at the Early Bronze III settlement of Numeira (McCreery, 1980). Comparing results with the spectrum of present natural flora from the Dead Sea province, McCreery considered that climatic changes during the past 5,000 years were not sufficient to alter substantially wild plant life of the region. This should relate only to most of Early Bronze and the present but not to Middle and Late Bronze. Information from the entire region clearly indicates that, in addition to the mild Climatic Wet Subphase II-b sometime within Early Bronze, a much wetter subphase occurred after the Intermediate Bronze age. These data were derived from studies of the Uvda Valley, Jericho, the Sea of Galilee (mostly Beth Yerah), the Beth She'an basin, south Syria, and north Mesopotamia, supported by data from the caves of Mount Sedom and coreholes of the south basin. Numeira and Bab edh-Dhr'a are just 22 km and 14 km from the caves and from coreholes where effects of a climatic wet phase are very pronounced. Paleobotanical evidence such as that studied by McCreery could not have been collected from archaeological layers of the post–Intermediate Bronze age at either Numeira or Bab edh-Dhr'a because post–Intermediate Bronze and pre-Hellenistic sedimentary sequences there are barren of archaeological remains, including agricultural ones. Transgressive lake sediments of Climatic Wet Phase III were not deposited at the top of these two settlements at elevations of −220 and −280 m m.s.l., higher than the uppermost levels of the sea (−300 m m.s.l.) in post–Intermediate Bronze or Middle to Late Bronze transgressions.

McCreery's data by themselves are instructive from another perspective; they indicate that the assemblage of cultigen products went through gradual environmental changes between Early Bronze I and Early Bronze IV. During that time span a shift occurred from equal amounts of wheat and barley with important contributions of flax and legumes to dominance of barley and a severe decline to even total disappearance of other crops. McCreery considered that such a change could have occurred only because of gradual increase in soil salinity caused by long continuous irrigation of cultigens with available slightly brackish spring water. A gradually increasing amount of boron was detected in all such irrigated Early Bronze crop specimens from Numeira and Bab edh-Dhr'a. Their boron contents are systematically larger than those in modern wheat and barley samples collected near Karak, 15 km farther east on the Jordanian plateau, so a gradual worsening of the problem of soil salinity during the entire Early Bronze age is supported.

Dating of Wet Subphase II-b (Figure 3.2 and Table 3.3) as Early Bronze II agrees with the following sequence of events. South basin was first settled by the time of Early Bronze I age about 5000 B.P., and developed uninterruptedly until the end of Early Bronze. Unlike the city of Arad, availability of plentiful subsurface water at Numeira and Bab edh-Dhr'a enabled them to survive for an additional few hundred years in spite of gradually increasing drought, destructive earthquakes, and cultural pressure of raids and conquests. This survival continued only until the drought became too extreme by about 4200 B.P.

Mount Sedom Caves

Data from Mount Sedom caves (Frumkin et al., 1991; Figure 3.4) emphasize the unique climatic conditions of post–Intermediate Bronze IV age or of Climatic Wet Phase III by supplying information on high-level Dead Sea transgressions and their durations. Radiocarbon ages of 33 wood samples collected from the caves range from 7100 to about 200 B.P. Age distribution is fairly uniform except for clustering of six samples within a 400-year span, 4600 to 4200 B.P. Four of these six are fossil oak-wood samples from galleries or passages in three different caves whose outlets now hang along a horizontal line at an elevation of about −360 m m.s.l. and above the base of the East fault escarpment of Mount Sedom. The galleries and these oak twigs probably date from this same wet phase. Chimney openings of these caves are near the

−300 m m.s.l. contour. Most hollowed spaces of chimneys and galleries subsequently became filled to their ceilings and upper openings with detrital sediments, mostly fragmented aragonite laminae from Lisan Formation at the top of Mount Sedom. Similar detrital sediments with occasional plant remains were deposited within older and younger caves but included no fragments of oak.

The 29 other fossil plant fragments from the caves attest that all belonged to the same semiarid botanical community (*Anabasis retifera* Moq, *Haloxylon persicum, Tamarix* sp.) that still grows beside the Dead Sea, which is devoid of oak trees. Frumkin et al. (1991) suggested that at a certain stage during Climatic Wet Phase III the sea rose quite rapidly, submerging outlets of the caves at −360 m m.s.l. and reaching the tops of their chimneys at −300 m m.s.l. Outlets and galleries of the submerged caves became plugged with detrital sediments in which the oak fragments were buried. They had been swept into the openings of the chimneys either by local floodwaters from the limited catchment area on Mount Sedom or by longshore currents when the level was that high. Oak trees could have grown locally or in the much larger catchment area of the surrounding province from which they would have been flushed by flood waters into the sea. "Oak does not grow today in the Dead Sea area as it needs more than 500 mm annual precipitation" (Frumkin et al. 1991, p. 196, quoting A. Danin of Hebrew University, personal communication).

Kinneret Plain

Kinneret Plain is the exposed south part of the Sea of Galilee basin (Figures 1.2, 4.1, 4.2) that contains archaeological sites, the most important of which is Tel Beth Yerah. Data from there and from the Beth She'an basin indicate the presence of two significant wet phases during Holocene, the earlier one during Pre-Pottery Neolithic B age (PPNB)—8300 to 7800 B.P. (Bar-Yosef and Mintz, 1979). The later one, Climatic Wet Phase III, followed the break between Early and Middle Bronze and lasted from about 3900 B.P. until the end of Late Bronze, about 3200 B.P. Even the top of Tel Beth Yerah (Figure 4.1) near the southwest corner of the Sea of Galilee and the present outlet through the Jordan River at an elevation of −190 m m.s.l. was transgressed during that phase.

Climatic fluctuations during Lisan Lake time, the Würm glacial stage of Late Pleistocene and the transition to Holocene, 25,000 to 8000 B.P., are expressed at Tel Beth Yerah by upward facies changes and archaeological remains of habitation within the sedimentary sequence cropping out along its precipitous 20-m-high flanks. The sequence here consists of several layers. At the east base of the tel is a relatively thick bluish green layered marl much of which has been penetrated by shallow drill

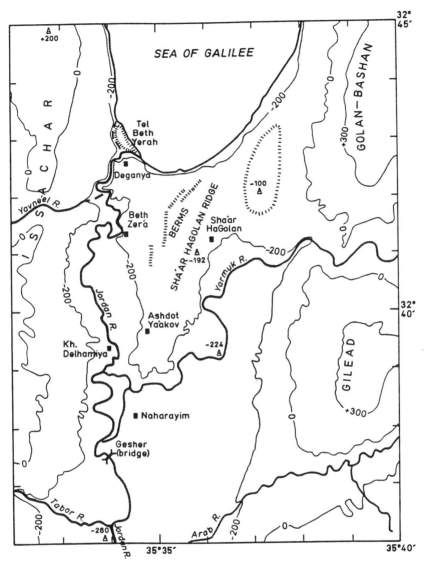

Figure 4.1. Physiographic map of Kinneret Plain and on-land south part of the Sea of Galilee basin showing segments of paleoberms trending north-northeast to northeast composed mostly of carbonate sand grains along west flank of the low Sha'ar HaGolan Ridge. Steep and high relief areas to the East and West are border fault escarpments of the graben and are shown by 100-m contours. In the lowlands elevations of some triangulation points supplement information from contours.

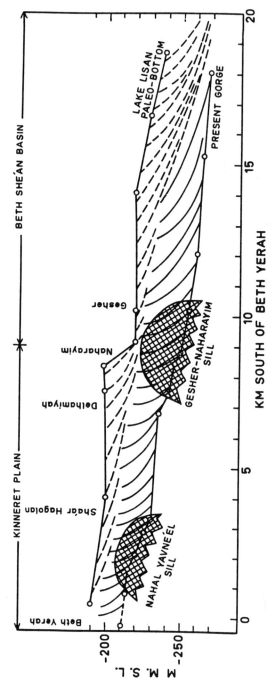

Figure 4.2. Entrenchment of the Jordan River indicated by comparing two superimposed longitudinal (north-south) topographic profiles made along trough of Kinneret Plain and north part of Beth She'an basin. Upper profile is paleobottom of Lisan Lake; lower one is bed of the Jordan River. Two paleosills are identified. The south one separates Kinneret and Beth She'an basins and consists of an 800,000-year-old basalt flow that reached Gesher-Naharayim area from the Golan Heights along present gorge of the Yarmuk River. North sill consists of erosion-resistant alluvial-gravel beds of Nahal (river) Yavne'el's delta. Another bridge (Kanatir) was built by Romans at that site. Steeper river gradients occur down the flow line at the sills and fords.

78

holes. A campsite of early Kebaran fisher-hunter-gatherers having a radiocarbon age of 19,000 B.P. and a very early Epipaleolithic age occasionally became exposed during times of low lake level at –212.2 m m.s.l. (Nadel, 1991; Nadel and Hershkovitz, 1991). The next layer is a 17,000-year old bed of fine-grained gravels and sands with wide distribution and thickness between 1 and 4 m (Neev, 1978). The third unit is a 2-m layer of typical Lisan facies deposited during climatic cycle 8 of the Würm stage (Table 3.3; Figures 3.2, 3.6). In places this layer underwent a syndepositional process similar to slumps at Perazim Canyon west of Mount Sedom (Figure 2.12), indicating tectonic movement or eastward tilt during that time. Large gypsum crystals and smaller rosette-shaped ones are abundant in this uppermost Lisan-facies layer. A thin layer of yellowish white sandy-to-gravelly marl separates the Lisan Formation from overlying swamp sediments.

At Tel Beth Yerah and Kinneret Plain, the Lisan Formation is overlain by a layer of archaeologically sterile dark-brown swamp sediments several meters thick, deposited during the Natufian to Pre-Pottery Neolithic ages in the Pleistocene-Holocene transition—12,500 to 8000 B.P. (Bar-Yosef and Mintz, 1979; Schuldenrein and Goldberg, 1981; Macumber and Head, 1991).

Natufian to Neolithic swamps existed as independent shallow-water bodies at various elevations within and along the Jordan Valley (Neev and Emery, 1967; Begin et al., 1974). Within the Kinneret Plain the thickness of these swamp sediments increases from the Yarmuk River delta toward a north-south-trending depression, 8 km long and 3 km wide, along the west flank of that plain (N. Nammeri, soil expert, personal communication). It was formed by tectonic subsidence adjacent to the West border fault of the graben. Later the Jordan River gorge became entrenched along the depression's axis (Figures 4.1, 4.2). The layer of swamp sediments wedges out and interfingers with gravel beds east within the Yarmuk delta as well as west within the delta of Nahal (river) Yavne'el. Detrital components of these sediments came mostly from the Yarmuk River because the north part of the Sea of Galilee is continuously subsiding and forms a settling basin that traps most sediments from the upper Jordan region.

Earliest evidence of human habitation of Tel Beth Yerah during the Holocene is from Early Bronze I, about 5000 B.P. This cultural layer unconformably overlies swamp sediments of Neolithic age at elevations near –200 m m.s.l. An uninterrupted sequence continues upward from Early Bronze I to the end of Early Bronze III, when the site was conquered, destroyed, and burned by Early Bronze IV (Intermediate Bronze) people, who immediately resettled it. An abrupt cultural break associated with an unconformable erosional surface overlies the entire tel above the Early Bronze IV layer beginning about 4200 B.P. It began the abandonment of this site during the next 1,500 years until Hellenistic times (Mazar, Stekelis, and Avi-Yonah, 1952; Bar-Adon, 1956, 1957; Kochavi, 1973–1974; Neev, 1978; Esse, 1982; Hestrin, 1993; E. Eisenberg, personal communication). Shallow erosional channels in that surface were filled later with a badly sorted but clean mixture of pebbles and sand mixed with sherds of Early Bronze pottery, some of which have rounded edges from stream erosion, as well as with shells of freshwater mollusks (*Melanopsis* sp. and *Unio* sp.). A layer with a maximum thickness of 1 m with homogeneous yellowish to tan silty clays changing facies laterally into gravel and sand lenses overlies this material.

The granules, minerals, and color of these youngest sediments resemble those of recent well-aerated lake deposits in the southwest shoals of the Sea of Galilee east of its outlet. At least one articulated bivalve (*Unio* sp.) was found in burrowing position within this post–Early Bronze IV mud layer indicating a natural aquatic environment of deposition. Radiocarbon age of 5400 ± 180 B.P. was determined for a single valve of *Unio* sp. found nearby within the same layer (Neev, 1978). The discrepancy in ages between the appreciably older single shell and the archaeologically based post–Early Bronze IV (4200 B.P.) unconformity can best be explained by an apparent high radiocarbon age of seawater contributed by dead carbon. This problem is similar to age discrepancies in the Dead Sea south basin, Mount Sedom caves, and Beth She'an basin.

The settlement at Tel Beth Yerah of Early Bronze IV or the Intermediate Bronze ages probably was deserted after 4200 B.P. not because of conquest but because of submergence under flooding water of the Sea of Galilee. Evidently, sometime after 3900 B.P. or after the Intermediate Bronze age, the level of the sea rose at least 10 m from about –200 m, the elevation of the Early Bronze I layer, to –190 m m.s.l. because of climatic change from relatively dry to wet. A tectonic subsidence factor for the transgression is excluded because the sea level also would tend to drop and not rise if the basin subsided tectonically. Wet climatic regime may have lasted for a relatively long time, perhaps a few centuries, depending on its causes. No indication of flooding was found at Tel Beth Yerah in younger post–Hellenic times.

Most entrenchment of the Jordan and Yarmuk River gorges occurred during Wet Subphase I-a and Climatic Wet Phase III (Table 3.3). Although these were cumulative, their individual amounts of energy spent per meter depth of erosion could have been different. The reason lies in the vertical lithological changes in both the Gesher-Naharayim sill (Figures 4.1, 4.2, 4.3, 4.4) and the Beth She'an basin's south sill that were breached. Upper halves at the sills consist of soft, easily eroded sediments of the Lisan Formation; the lower half of the former is dense basalt and that of the latter cemented conglomerate.

The rise in level of the Sea of Galilee during the two wet phases of Pre-Pottery Neolithic B and the Middle Bronze ages flooded the entire basin including most of the Kinneret Plain, creating a water body south

Figure 4.3. Basalt flow within the Yarmuk River near its junction with the Jordan River. A Roman bridge in use until 1948 and a recent dam were built on the basalt. The flow forms the sill between Kinneret Plain and Beth She'an basin (Figure 4.2).

RUINED BRIDGE OF SEMAKH.

Figure 4.4. Kanatir Bridge (Lynch, 1849) 1 km south of Beth Yerah built by Romans on deltaic conglomerates of Nahal Yavne'el (Figures 4.1, 4.2).

of Mount Hermon similar to the Huleh Lake swamp prior to about 1950. The plain was topographically higher than the similar water body on its south, the Beth She'an basin. During intensive wet phases, water from the Sea of Galilee flowed south like a huge river through the depressed belt on the west side of the plain. After the first entrenchment event in Pre-Pottery Neolithic B, the Yarmuk gorge stopped flowing west from the mountains when the newly incised gorge was deflected southwest to join the Jordan River at Gesher-Naharayim (Figures 4.1, 4.2). The west part of Kinneret Plain then became detached from the main source of coarse-grained sediment in the east. The north-northeast-trending Sha'ar HaGolan Ridge crosses the plain separating the two rivers. Its highest point at −192 m m.s.l. is 8 m above the average elevation of the plain.

When the Sea of Galilee flooded the Kinneret Plain, its east shoreline stretched north-south along the west flanks of the Sha'ar HaGolan Ridge. Remains of this shoreline have the form of three individual segments of an approximately 3-km-long north-south-trending berm, the central point of which is at Latitude 32°41′20″N, Longitude 35°35′00″E (Figure 4.1). The central segment is the most pronounced and has been most thoroughly studied. This ridge, 1.5 km long, 50 m wide, and nearly 1 m high, is composed of well-sorted carbonate sand particles along the −195 m m.s.l. contour line, extending north for about 1 km, where its trend bends northeast. A very shallow 200-m-wide trough borders its east side (A. Kinnarti, soil expert, personal communication). The other two segments lie *en echelon* southwest and northeast of the central one. All three segments are relicts of sequential berms formed along transgressing or regressing shores of a south tongue of the sea. That sea existed in post–Neolithic ages because the berms overlie swamp sediments deposited during the Natufian and Early Neolithic ages. Perhaps during Climatic Wet Phase III, the level of the sea in Middle to Late Bronze was even higher than that of its berms (−195 m m.s.l.), as indicated by the elevation of its sediments (−190 m m.s.l.) at Tel Beth Yerah.

During the Natufian and Early Neolithic ages, the outlet of the Jordan River from the Sea of Galilee was at the Gesher-Naharayim sill about 10 km south of Tel Beth Yerah where the present gorges of the Jordan and Yarmuk Rivers meet (Figure 4.1). An 0.8-million-year-old lava flow underlies the soft Lisan sequence at that site (Figures 4.2, 4.3), indicating that the flow reached at least that far on its course from the Golan volcanic belt through the Yarmuk River gorge into the Jordan graben, where it built a dam across the Jordan Valley (Picard, 1932; Mor and Steinitz, 1985). Excessive accumulation of chemical and detrital sediments within Lisan Lake and the Early Neolithic swamp was caused by the damming effect of the Gesher-Naharayim sill shaping Kinneret Plain. Farther south the depositional plain of Beth She'an basin, 30 to 40 m topographically lower, was formed by similar processes.

The Jordan and Yarmuk Rivers were entrenched into Kinneret Plain and both crossed the Gesher-Naharayim sill for the first time during Holocene Wet Substage I-a, or the Pre-Pottery Neolithic B age, 8500 to 7800 B.P. That age is indicated by the presence of a Pottery Neolithic settlement within the Yarmuk River gorge at an elevation of –214 to –216 m m.s.l., about 10 m above the present riverbed and 20 m below its bank at the paleodelta near Sha'ar HaGolan (Latitude 32°40'45", Longitude 35°36'25"E). This site later was buried under a 1-m-thick alluvial blanket deposited during Climatic Wet Phases II-a and III. It was excavated by Stekelis (1992) between 1943 and 1952, by Garfinkel (1990, 1993, and personal communication), and by Eisenberg (1993).

Intermediate Terrace was identified not only within the Yarmuk River gorge near Sha'ar HaGolan but also at two other large sites along the Jordan gorge within Kinneret Plain. The first is near Kibbutz Beth Zer'a on the east side of the river about 4 km south of Tel Beth Yerah (Figure 4.1). Chalcolithic and Early Bronze I and II settlements were identified within a terrace at an elevation of –210 to –215 m m.s.l., a few meters above the present bed of the river (Z. Vinogradov, local archaeologist, personal communication). A second large Chalcolithic site was identified at Khirbet Delhamiya a few kilometers downstream on a small hill about 25 m above the Jordan gorge (R. Amiran, 1977) also at an elevation of –215 m m.s.l. near the Gesher-Naharayim sill (Figures 4.1, 4.2). Nir and Ben-Arieh (1965) coined the term Intermediate Terrace and assumed that it was formed by a high level of the Dead Sea during a subpluvial interval between 11,500 and 10,000 B.P. or during the Natufian age (Tables 3.3, 3.4). That may be questionable because this terrace has a depositional origin and consists of fluviatile, swamp, and freshwater sediments and not of evaporite deposits as would be expected from highly saline although diluted brines of the Dead Sea or Lisan Lake. Its date of deposition is post–Late Neolithic and prior to Early Bronze or close to 6000 B.P.

Average elevations of Intermediate Terrace in Kinneret Plain and Beth She'an basin are appreciably different, –215 m and –265 m m.s.l. respectively. These were very near the local bottoms as well as the water levels of these two intermediate lakes. During most of Climatic Phase II, the level of the Dead Sea was probably about –400 m m.s.l. so that precipitous morphologic steps would have had to separate these three basins. Intermediate Terrace could not have been formed by a common base level of deposition along a single lake that would have had to stretch then between the Sea of Galilee and the Dead Sea.

Schuldenrein and Goldberg (1981, p. 67) suggested that the intensive regional erosional regime of Holocene began only after the Chalcolithic age on the basis of data from the Salibiya and Gilgal sites at the northwest flank of the lower Jordan Valley. Data from Kinneret Plain makes it more probable that this erosional event occurred a few thousand years earlier, about 8000 B.P. near the end of Wet Subphase I-a or Pre-Pottery Neolithic B (Figure 3.6; Table 3.3).

During Early Roman to Byzantine times, elevation of the Jordan River gorge at its outlet from the Sea of Galilee was about –208 m m.s.l. This estimate is based on identical elevation of a small damming structure built during the Roman or Early Byzantine time at the present east-west-trending outlet of the river just south of Tel Beth Yerah, presumably to prevent a new gorge from being incised then as actually occurred about 1,000 years later. The old outlet is near the north end of the north-south-trending segment of the now-abandoned riverbed at the northwest corner of Tel Beth Yerah. It joins the newly breached gorge at the south end of that segment about 1 km farther south (Picard, 1932; Bar-Adon, 1956; Ben-Arieh, 1965). Assuming that by Early Bronze IV the level of the Sea of Galilee was about –200 m m.s.l. near the contact between the Neolithic swamp and Early Bronze I layers, the gorge deepened about 8 m between –200 and –208 m m.s.l. near Tel Beth Yerah during the 2,000 years between Early Bronze IV and the Roman Age. Because of exceptional wetness of Climatic Wet Phase III, most of this entrenchment occurred during the first eight centuries of that time span. Additional deepening of only 4 m from –208 m to –212 m m.s.l. happened during the 1,700 years between Late Roman time and 1930 A.D., when a modern dam was built at the river outlet.

Erosion of the sills between basins generally was more intense during wet climatic phases than dry ones. In contrast, lake bottoms can be entrenched only during dry climates when they are exposed to subaerial processes. Much of Lisan Lake's bottom area was exposed after the last glacial wet phase of Pleistocene when its level gradually dropped. The two sills at south ends of the Sea of Galilee and the Beth She'an basin (Figures 1.2, 2.17, 4.1, 4.2) were breached during Wet Subphase I-a and Climatic Wet Phase III of Holocene (9000 to 7800 B.P. and 3900 to 3200 B.P., Table 3.3). The first breaching event would have been the normal headward erosional process caused by high dynamic gradients behind the sills at the north ends of intermediate lakes. Flooding of the paleo-depositional plains in these two basins, especially during Climatic Wet Phase III beginning about 3900 B.P., is difficult to visualize because many channels that drained into intermediate lakes already had been entrenched through the two sills during the earlier wet subphase.

Some information on recent similar flooding of the lower floodplain of the Jordan River within Beth She'an basin (Figure 4.5) is available. The width of this plain averages nearly 1 km along the central part of that basin, but it gradually narrows southward to less than 100 m near the south sill. During floods the flow through that sill was greater than normal when the resulting higher water level may have created small short-lived intermediate lakes. During Climatic Wet Phase III areal dimensions of these lakes increased and water level rose so that even the

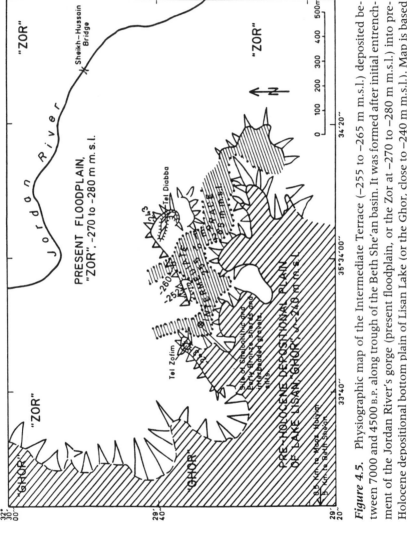

Figure 4.5. Physiographic map of the Intermediate Terrace (−255 to −265 m m.s.l.) deposited between 7000 and 4500 B.P. along trough of the Beth She'an basin. It was formed after initial entrenchment of the Jordan River's gorge (present floodplain, or the Zor at −270 to −280 m m.s.l.) into pre-Holocene depositional bottom plain of Lisan Lake (or the Ghor, close to −240 m m.s.l.). Map is based on data from an unpublished 1 : 5000 topographic map (2-m contour interval) by Pantomap, Jerusalem, 1979 (courtesy of A. Ya'akobi, Kibbutz Ma'oz Haiim), and Nir and Ben-Arieh (1965).

now hanging depositional plain of Lisan Lake, locally named Ghor, about 40 m above the Zor became flooded.

The process of coastal abrasion, especially prominent along the south shore of the Sea of Galilee, also is related indirectly to entrenchment of the Jordan River's outlet. Until recently before coastal protection measures were taken, the rate of southward shore recession was as much as 0.5 m per year primarily by abrasion of waves against the 10-m-high cliff of Lisan sediments along the south bight of the sea (Picard, 1932; Ben-Arieh, 1965). It is assumed that the rate of recession was at least temporarily reduced after the drop in the level of the sea from about –190 m to –212 m m.s.l. after Climatic Wet Phase III. The recent artificial damming system of the river's outlet produced a relatively stable level of the Sea of Galilee and maintained the intensity of shoreline abrasional processes. Apparently breaching at the new river gorge outlet after Roman-Byzantine times was enhanced by percolation of water through an east-west-trending tectonic fracture at the south flank of Tel Beth Yerah.

Multidisciplinary study of Late Holocene sediments was made on a 5-m core from the bottom of the Sea of Galilee at a water depth of 25 m (Stiller et al., 1983–84). Changes in depositional environments noted throughout this sequence were analyzed for diatoms, nonsiliceous algae, pollen, carbon and oxygen isotopic ratios, and iron-to-manganese ratio. Four radiocarbon age determinations were made on disseminated organic carbon contents of mud samples to estimate rates of deposition and compaction. Results allow no clear-cut correlation with known climatic changes in the region during the past 5,000 years. Most surprising is the absence of evidence for Climatic Wet Phase III. Indicators for three prominent ecological events were found in the younger part of that core. Both planktonic and benthonic (living on the bottom) diatoms were the main constituents of the lake's total phytoplankton biomass in the lower part of the core between 5000 and 2300 B.P. This population disappeared within a depth interval of 2.9 to 2.4 m or in a period between about 2300 to 1600 B.P. but renewed itself after the end of that break. Green algae abruptly increased both in abundance and diversity above a depth of 3.2 m or since about 2400 B.P.

Another peculiarity was an increase of about 50% in pollen within the upper part of that core from the Sea of Galilee at depths between 3.2 and 1.8 m. Within that depth range an increase of about 50% in the population of *Olea* (olive) capsules and a corresponding decrease of *Quercus* sp. (oak) were recorded. Radiocarbon age analyses indicate that the increase in *Olea* peaked about 2000 B.P. (Stiller et al., 1983–84, fig. 3), implying onset of a drier warmer climate (A. Horowitz, 1979). It could be understood that the *Olea* peak is well correlated with the warm dry period of the Roman age between Climatic Wet Subphases IV-a and IV-b (Table 3.3; Neumann, 1991, 1992). Stiller et al. considered that this increase in *Olea*-to-*Quercus* ratio was caused by cultural-economic human change—an increase in olive production rather than a climatic one. Issar et al. (1989) arrived at an even more complicated interpretation of the same data, saying that the increase reflects a climatic shift from warm dry conditions to more humid colder ones.

Beth She'an Basin

Climatically induced depositional-erosional events similar to those of Kinneret Plain and the Dead Sea south basin also are present in the Beth She'an basin (Figures 1.2, 4.5, 4.6). This nearly 30-km-long area extends from the Gesher-Naharayim basalt sill in the north to the sill-forming gravel bed of Miocene period at the Marma Feiyad-Tel en Naqra area (Schulman, 1978; Shaliv, Mimram, and Hatzer, 1992). A Late Pleistocene to Early Holocene fill at the center of that basin is dominated at its top by archaeologically sterile Natufian–Early Neolithic and later swamp sediments overlying Lisan-type soft marls and gypsiferous evaporites. The width of the basin increases from about 5 km at the north sill to 8 km near its middle, east of Beth She'an city (Figures 4.6, 4.7), south from which it narrows again to 5 km near the south sill. Elevation of the upper plain along the basin's trough is practically identical with that of the bottom of Lisan Lake; it gradually drops from –230 m m.s.l. at the north to –243 m m.s.l. at its center. Farther south the same elevation is maintained as far as approaches to the south sill. In contrast, the recent gorge of the Jordan River gradually drops from an elevation of –250 m m.s.l. to deeper than –300 m m.s.l. near the south sill (Figures 4.2, 4.5, 4.6). The reason for this considerable meandering of the river only 10 km south of the north sill (Schattner, 1962; topographic map of Israel Survey 1:50,000, 1972) should be studied further.

After the end of the Pre-Pottery Neolithic B age of Wet Subphase I-a (Tables 3.3, 3.4) Lisan Lake shrank, leaving behind hanging ponds and swamps. The Jordan River gorge became entrenched into the bottom sediment of that basin known as the Upper Terrace, forming most of the escarpment that separates the upper paleodepositional plain from the lower floodplain. The more than 1-km-wide lower erosional terrace of the Jordan Valley is similar to the recent floodplain of the river, which also was formed during that time. The Intermediate Terrace was formed during Wet Subphase II-a or Early to Mid-Chalcolithic. The recent floodplain, Zor, dates from further entrenchment a few more meters into the terrace. Elevations of the terrace drop sharply south across the step that separates Kinneret Plain and the north part of the Beth She'an basin from –216 m at Sha'ar HaGolan to –237 m at Tel Shoshan near the junction of the Tabor and Jordan rivers (Latitude 32°36'15", Longitude 35°33'55"E; Figures 4.1, 4.5). Farther south this

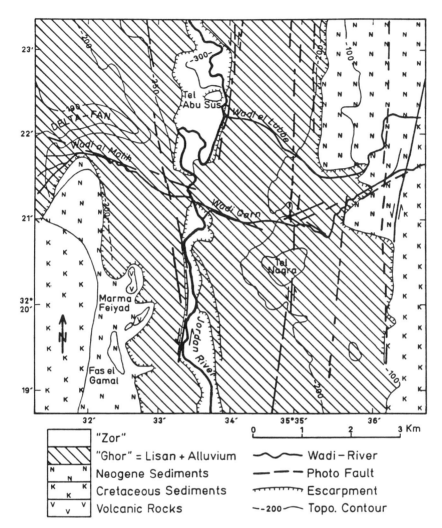

Figure 4.6. Physiographic-geologic sketch map of south sill area of the Beth She'an basin (after Schulman and Rosenthal, 1968). Photolineaments of tectonic origin were added. Thick gravel beds of Miocene to Pleistocene periods are especially abundant within the graben near the sill. Miocene gravel beds dip steeply east along photolineament that parallels the Jordan River just east of Tel Abu Sus in the north and Marma Feiyad in the south. This and other photolineaments farther east are components of the north-south-trending wrench fault system of the Jordan–Dead Sea system. The floodplain of the Jordan River appreciably narrows upon approaching the sill at the transverse tectonic lineament of Wadi al Malikh-Wadi Qarn and along it.

terrace gradually drops to –260 m, –268 m, and –275 m m.s.l. east of
Beth She'an city (Nir and Ben-Arieh, 1965, table 1).

An outcrop of Intermediate Terrace at the central part of the Beth
She'an basin is described here in some detail because these data are important for establishing origin and age. This is near the foot of the escarpment between the Ghor and the Zor just east of Kibbutz Maoz Haiyim
between elevations of –261 and –265 m m.s.l. (Latitude 32°29′35″, Longitude 35°33′50″; Figure 4.5). The several-meter-thick sequence of alternating carbonate tufa-coated and cemented gravel beds and marl layers
rich in Chalcolithic pottery sherds is overlain by a soil horizon containing uncoated Early Bronze I sherds comprising the upper few meters of
Intermediate Terrace. These sherd-bearing layers were investigated by
A. Ya'akobi, a local archaeologist who found and studied this site. Distribution of these sherds led to the suggestion that they are very near the
site of a Chalcolithic settlement. All detrital components of that sequence,
excluding the uppermost Early Bronze I layer, are heavily coated with
tufa enclosing freshwater gastropod shells, *Melanopsis* sp., indicating their
former submergence in a shallow freshwater pond saturated with cal-
cium carbonate. These sherds were deposited just within the Zor about
6000 B.P. during Climatic Wet Subphase II-a or during Ghassulian age of
the Early to Mid-Chalcolithic and prior to Early Bronze I.

A cultural sequence of Chalcolithic to Intermediate Bronze settlements unconformably overlain by Iron and Roman age pottery sherds
was found at the east edge of the upper terrace, the Ghor, at the top of
Tel Zofim about 20 m higher and just 200 m west of the Intermediate
Terrace outcrop at Maoz Haiyim (Figure 4.5; Zori, 1962, p. 155; Neev,
1978; A. Ya'akobi, personal communication). Tufa deposits that enclose
freshwater gastropod shells also coat and cement many Intermediate
Bronze age pottery sherds at this site but are not present on the underlying Chalcolithic or the overlying Iron and Roman sherds. A climatically
induced rise of water level that submerged even the upper terrace at this
relatively high topographic site of –243 m m.s.l. meant creation of a water
body more than 20 m deep in the Beth She'an basin sometime during
post–Intermediate Bronze prior to the Iron age. More precisely this event
probably occurred about 3,900 years ago. Two radiocarbon age analyses
made on duplicate *Melanopsis* sp. samples from that tufa deposit of Tel
Zofim yielded ages of 4400 ± 200 B.P. and 5000 ± 400 B.P. (W. S. Broecker,
personal communication, 1964; Neev and Emery, 1967, p. 28). This difference between radiocarbon and traditional archaeological chronology
for the same climatic event during Middle Bronze II to Late Bronze time
is analogous to that inferred from coreholes of the Dead Sea south basin
and Mount Sedom caves with respect to Bab edh-Dhr'a and Tel Beth
Yerah sites. These data also confirm the conclusion about initial entrenchment of the Jordan River during Holocene after the transition from the
Early to the Late Neolithic ages (Table 3.4).

Middle Bronze II sherds at several sites on the upper terrace, Ghor, within the Beth She'an basin at elevations near –240 m (Zori, 1962) suggest that the water level of the post–Intermediate Bronze lake in that basin did not reach much higher than that. Apparently most detailed physiography within the basin already was shaped prior to Climatic Wet Phase III (Table 3.3).

According to Koucky and Smith (1986) a freshwater body continued within the Beth She'an basin (Beisan Lake) long after the retreat of Lisan Lake. They proposed that the highest level of that lake reached –100 m m.s.l. during Natufian time, 12,000 to 11,000 B.P., gradually receding through the Neolithic and Chalcolithic ages until its disappearance by Early Bronze. Although relict ponds could have been preserved above the highest level along the graben's border faults, such a proposal is questionable for several reasons. Relict spots of the youngest depositional plain of the lake containing genuine Lisan-like sediments are traced across the Beth She'an basin as far as its south sill (Marma Feiyad-Tel en Naqra; Figure 4.6) at elevations near –240 m m.s.l. These clearly indicate that the sill's elevation was never higher than –240 m m.s.l. The relatively old ages of the Gesher-Naharayim basalt flow during Early to Mid-Pleistocene and of the gravel bed at Marma Feiyad during Miocene (Schulman and Rosenthal, 1968) show that they functioned as sills across the Jordan Valley since Mid-Pleistocene. Steeply tilted Miocene gravel beds along the Jordan River near Marma Feiyad reveal that tectonic deformation preceded deposition of overlying horizontal beds of the Lisan Formation. The water body of the intermediate lake in the Beth She'an basin could not have reached a level as high as –100 m m.s.l. and remained there for 1,000 years during Late Epipaleolithic (12,000 to 11,000 B.P.; Koucky and Smith, 1986, p. 29).

Similar data and arguments show that extensive travertine, marl, and silt deposits formed terraces and ponds just west of Beth She'an city at elevations of –100 to –120 m m.s.l (Figures 1.2, 4.5, 4.7). These sediments were deposited from slightly brackish waters still seeping at springs near the foot of Mount Gilbo'a. They could not have been deposited by the water bodies of Lisan Lake or contemporary Beisan Lake that flooded the entire Beth She'an basin. During the time span from earliest Chalcolithic to the present, most of the Ghor could not have been flooded by a 200-m-deep lake, as indicated by the distribution pattern of sites in both time and area. The ponds were very small, shallow, independent water bodies hanging above and draining into the Beth She'an basin.

Jericho

The first human settlement in Jericho was by Mesolithic people of the Natufian age, 12,500 to 10,300 B.P. (Table 3.4), following initial reces-

Figure 4.7.   Tel Beth She'an in 1959.

sion of the high-level Lisan Lake during Late Pleistocene. Evidence for that settlement is within and above a 30-cm clay layer of swamp environment at Tel Jericho (Tel es Sultan) overlying a Late Cretaceous chalky limestone subcrop (Kenyon, 1979, pp. 22–24). A 20-m-high mound, most of which is a sequence of human occupational sediments accumulated before the end of the Late Bronze, forms an elongate north-south tel about 8 hectars (150 × 550 m) in extent. The perennial fresh water (Cl = 30 ppm) Elisha Spring named for the prophet who "purified" it (2 Kings 2:19–22) flows from the eastern foot of the tel (Figures 4.8, 4.9, 4.10, 4.11, 4.12) at an elevation of about –200 m m.s.l.

Tectonics and physiography of Tel Jericho and its vicinity were important factors in its cultural history. The 1:50,000 geological map of Jericho (Begin, 1974; personal communication) delineates well-proven faults as continuous lines in Figure 4.8 as well as the distribution pattern of outcropping stratigraphic units. Several faults and lineaments inferred from aerial photographs and other information were added to the sketch map as dashed lines. The Samia fault branches to the left from the main north-south-trending west border fault of the Dead Sea graben at a point west of Tel Jericho. This pattern is similar to many other crescentic faults that branch from the main graben (Picard, 1943; Ilani and Mimran, 1982).

The Tel Jericho West fault gradually curves clockwise (Begin, 1974) to merge with the south fault of Wadi Nu'eima that trends east-west. The East fault is a photolineament along the east side of Tel Jericho, extending north and gradually curving clockwise parallel with the West fault to merge with the Wadi Nu'eima south fault. Late Cretaceous chalky bedrock crops out not only just north of Tel Jericho but was excavated beneath the archaeological sequence within the tel's limits. Prolific freshwater of the Spring of Elisha (Figure 4.13) rises probably from deeply buried cavernous reservoir rocks of this age fed by rainfall on the Judean Mountains. These waters probably ascend through channels along fractured rocks of the East fault. This is at a place where "the surface of the rock [that] sloped gently down from the west . . . flattens off into the alluvial plain of the valley-bed" (Kenyon, 1979, pp. 22–24). The downthrown sides of the Tel Jericho faults, both East and West, are on their east so they appear to be step faults dropping toward the trough of the main rift.

The East and West normal faults at the east periphery of the Nu'eima Block trend from north-northeast to south-southwest and drop to the east (Begin, 1974; Fig. 4.8). Originally they may have extended south to join the Tel Jericho East and West faults as continuous lines. Their present pattern suggests that they were shifted horizontally a few hundred meters during a later deformation caused by an east-west-trending strike-slip fault zone along Wadi Nu'eima. This zone is expressed on several *en echelon* photolineaments. Its existence is supported by the sys-

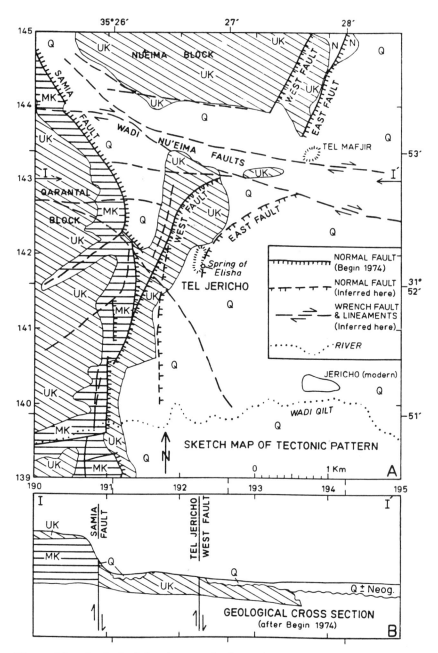

Figure 4.8. Geological sketch map of Tel Jericho area and an east-west geological cross-section after Begin (1974). An independent interpretation of the tectonic pattern was made from study of photolineaments and their distribution (air-photographs courtesy of Pantomap, Jerusalem, as well as from field observations). That pattern has the following main features: (1) Mountainous Qarantal block composed mostly of Judean Group (Middle Cretaceous = MK, horizontal lining) dense dolomites and topped by soft marly chalks of the Mount Scopus Group (Late Cretaceous = LK, diagonal lining). It is limited on its east

tem of abundant transverse faults that cross Samaria as mapped by detailed surface surveys of Ilani and Mimran (1982). Mimran (1984,
fig. 2, and personal communication) showed the presence of a few hundred meters of dextral strike-slip movement across two of the east-west-
trending systems at the east flank of the Faria Anticline in northeast
Samaria. Sakal (1968) found that the upthrown block of such an east-
west-trending fault system in east Negev had been thrust north. Bartov
(1971, 1974) mapped a similar system in central north Sinai as dextral
strike-slip faults. Neev et al. (1976) related east-west-trending fault
systems in Sinai-Negev province to compression associated with crustal
shortening caused by northward movements of broad slices of plates
(Figure 1.1).

Close association of the east face of Tel Jericho with a major fault
carries practical geological implications—multiple destructions of the city
wall by earthquakes. In spite of occasional damage to its wall, the en-
closure of the spring secured abundant freshwater during times of conflict and the nearness to the tel of lush growth of agricultural products
had advantages for inhabitants.

The site of Jericho allowed physical control of the most important
route from the Jordanian highland, especially from the north and central provinces of Ammon and Gilead to Judea (Figure 1.2). Fifth-century
scholar Rabbi Samuel Bar-Nahmani (A.D. 426–500) described the strategic importance of Jericho in ancient times in the Midrash Rabba as
follows: "Jericho is the latch of the Land of Israel. If Jericho was taken
the whole country would instantly be conquered."

Occupational transition from Natufian into the Proto-Neolithic or
Pre-Pottery Neolithic A age at Jericho between 10,300 and 8300 B.P.
associated with relatively dry climate and gradual development from a
nomadic way of life into a settled and urban one was based on a suc-
cessful agricultural system including irrigation (Figure 3.6, Tables 3.3,
3.4; Bar-Yosef and Mintz, 1979; Kenyon, 1979). Massive defense facilities with solid stone walls and a round tower (Figure 4.12) were first

---

by the main West border fault of the Dead Sea graben that deviates northeast
to form the crescentic Samia fault (Picard, 1943; Ilani and Mimran, 1982).
(2) Nu'eima block in the north, limited on its south by Wadi Nu'eima transverse system of faults. (3) Two systems of north-south-trending normal step
faults formed along east flanks of Qarantal Block (Tel Jericho East and West
faults) and along Nu'eima block (Khirbet al Mafjir East and West faults).
(4) Nu'eima block, together with its two step faults evidently were shifted right
laterally along the dextral wrench fault system of Wadi Nu'eima with respect
to Qarantal block and both Tel Jericho step faults. Surface expressions of the
two step-fault systems suggest dextral or right-lateral movement along the
Nu'eima transverse fault system sometime in post-Miocene times. (5) The plain
east of Tels Jericho and Mafjir is covered by alluvium, congomerates, and marls
of the Dead Sea Group.

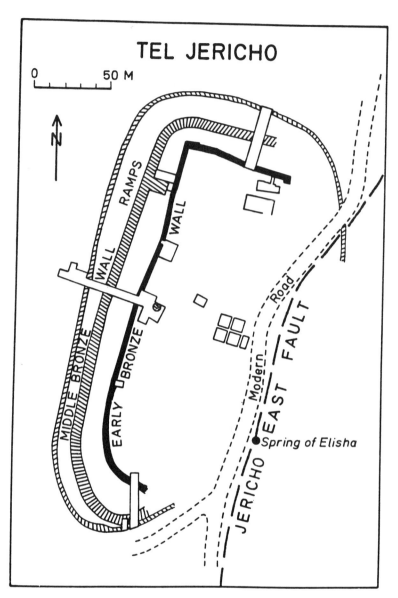

Figure 4.9. Sketch map of Tel Jericho (Kenyon, 1979, fig. 4, p. 23). Two city walls were excavated on the tel extending along its west (long) dimension as well as its north and south rims but not along the steepest east rim. Outer wall was built during Middle Bronze as a stable ramp or glacis. It extends south from northeast corner of the tel across the east slope and reaches the plain at the foot of the tel suggesting that originally it enclosed the Elisha Spring within defended limits of the Middle Bronze city. It is possible that similar defense concepts were employed by Early Bronze inhabitants so that the inner wall, or Early Bronze one, also enclosed water source for that city. No Late Bronze walls were found.

Figure 4.10. Cross-section of a mud-brick wall at Tel Hazor north of the Sea of Galilee and along the major strike-slip fault of the Dead Sea–Jordan rift—destroyed probably by an ancient earthquake.

Figure 4.11. Early Bronze west wall of Tel Jericho made of mud bricks and stones.

Figure 4.12. Early Neolithic (about 10,000 years old) cylindrical tower at Tel Jericho built of stones and mud.

Figure 4.13. Spring of Elisha at east side of Tel Jericho. Its water rises probably along a fault whose movements may have repeatedly destroyed the east
defensive wall.

built there about 10,000 B.P. and maintained until the end of Pre-Pottery
Neolithic A when heavy erosion occurred. By that time the site had been
abandoned apparently because of a change in climate to a more pluvial
one and possible flooding of irrigated lands east of the tel by the rising
level of Lisan Lake. The change was accompanied by initial entrenchment of the Jordan and Yarmuk rivers into Kinneret Plain, Beth She'an
basin, and Dead Sea basin. New people who settled in these areas ar-

rived from Syria with developed architecture of different origin and other characteristics of previous occupational culture. This new era, coined as Pre-Pottery Neolithic B, remained in Jericho for about 500 years (8300 to 7800 B.P.; Table 3.3). The new town was considerably larger than the largest Bronze one. Transition from Pre-Pottery Neolithic B to subsequent Pottery Neolithic was associated with an even more intensive erosional event followed by a long period of extremely dry climate and a cultural gap of 1,000 to 1,500 years. Pottery Neolithic occupation is divided into two subperiods, A and B, ending about 6700 B.P. (Gilead, 1993, table II). This age is considered primitive and regressive compared with Pre-Pottery Neolithic and later Ghassulian cultures (Kenyon, 1979).

Although Tel Jericho was not inhabited during Chalcolithic time, an industrial community of newcomers with Chalcolithic or Ghassulian culture settled at Tuleilat (hillocks in Arabic) Ghassul (Latitude 31°48′20″N; Longitude 35°36′10″E, elevation –290 m m.s.l.). Its remains are distributed over several mounds about 15 km southeast of Jericho and about 4 km east of Jordan River. A succession of farming communities whose inhabitants mastered highly developed copper metalwork, building, and artistic techniques occupied this site during Early to Middle Chalcolithic times. Although radiocarbon in occupational layers at that site as well as those of the same culture elsewhere in Israel ranged between 5700 and 5000 B.P., the calibrated age of its peak flourishing period is between 6300 and 6000 B.P. (Gilead, 1993).

Ghassulians appear to have arrived in Canaan from somewhere else in the Mideast after a hiatus at the end of the Pottery Neolithic age. Later they disappeared without indications of conquest or destruction of their settlements; they simply vanished. No relics of their occupation have ever been found just beneath any levels of Early Bronze cities in Canaan (Kenyon, 1979, pp. 52, 64). Apparently their occupational history was controlled by fluctuating climatic processes, a change from dry to wet climate during Wet Subphase II-a, returning to a dry subphase.

Transition from Chalcolithic to Proto-Urban or earliest Bronze cultures in Jericho during the last of the 3rd or 4th millennium B.C. was precipitated by invasion of new people from the east. These Proto-Urban immigrants did not bring with them a ready-made urban civilization but gradually developed and mastered one. Pronounced influence of Egyptian penetration is noticed mostly in Early Bronze sites of south Israel and north Sinai (Gilead, 1993). Based on pottery affinities and shaft-tomb practices, the occupational layer of the earliest settlers at Bab edh-Dhr'a was designated by Lapp (1968a, 1968b, 1970, as quoted by Rast and Schaub, 1978) as Early Bronze I-a dated between about 5150 and 5050 B.P. Altogether the nearly 1,000-year cultural history of Early Bronze at Jericho is similar to that at Bab edh-Dhr'a and Beth Yerah.

Jericho flourished after the beginning of Early Bronze I as a city that defended itself with mud-brick walls (Figure 4.10). The subsequent Early Bronze II city existed between 4900 and 4600 B.P. (Albright, 1965). Early Bronze III civilization extended between 4600 and 4350 B.P. Early Bronze defense walls were excavated at Jericho on the north, west, and south sides of the tel. Much of the east side has been destroyed by modern road construction so it is not certain that during this time the spring was enclosed (Figures 1.5, 4.8, 4.9). It seems, however, that "even at this stage the tel had a pronounced tilt downward to the east, probably because the buildings always sloped down toward the spring" (Kenyon, 1979, p. 90). City walls of unbaked mud brick collapsed several times as a result of earthquakes, with faces fallen forward onto ground level. Similar collapse at Tel Hazor is illustrated by Figure 4.10. The last Early Bronze III walls were built in a great hurry (Kenyon, 1979, p. 114) and indications were found of violent conflagrations apparently caused by attacking invaders.

The end of Early Bronze III in Jericho came with a terrible natural catastrophe followed by an invasion of nomads who settled there after the conquest but did not continue the life-style of the Early Bronze III civilization and did not take advantage of available remaining facilties. This culture is labeled by Rast and Schaub (1981) as Early Bronze IV and Middle Bronze I, extending between 4350 and 4200 B.P. Later, when its transitional nature was realized, the title was changed to Intermediate Bronze age.

The abrupt violent end of occupation occurring simultaneously at Bab edh-Dhr'a, Numeira, Jericho, and Beth Yerah also happened at about the same time at most other Early Bronze III sites in Israel and neighboring countries. Desertion of the entire region by Early Bronze IV people about 150 years later was not associated with violence or invasion and conquest. That cultural gap at Bab edh-Dhr'a and Beth Yerah was exceptionally long—1,500 years—and continued until Hellenistic time. At most other sites, including Jericho, these hiatuses were much shorter—200 to 300 years—or until sometime in Middle Bronze II, about 3900 B.P.

Early Bronze civilization survived in Jericho for almost 1,000 years. Younger parts of Early Bronze IV layers were eroded from Tel Jericho's summit, and silt and pottery sherd debris were redeposited within adjacent trenches at its foot. The intensity of that erosional event suggests a change into Climatic Wet Phase III (Table 3.3; Figures 3.1 and 3.2) that followed the Intermediate Bronze age.

Wet conditions of Climatic Phase III began with Middle Bronze II-a and ended at the close of Late Bronze in 3200 B.P. A highly developed Middle Bronze urban civilization at Jericho flourished as a city-state during a few hundred years until it was conquered and destroyed, apparently by Egyptians, in 3567 B.P.

During Middle Bronze II new inhabitants used an entirely different method of defense. The first version was city walls made of free-standing sun-dried bricks, such as characterized Early Bronze. The new type included the important element of artificial banks. The west bank at Jericho consisted of an earth ramp that sloped away both outside and inside and was built on bedrock. The ramp was more than 20 m wide with a low retaining stone base and was topped with a vertical wall reaching several meters higher (Kenyon, 1979, fig. 48, pp. 162–164). Apparently the architecture and engineering of this ramped structure were inspired by Hyksos technology. Unlike the single vertical wall of the Early Bronze defense, this one could escape collapse from earthquakes. These defenses enclosed Early Bronze walls on the city's north, west, and south sides and extended east beyond the steep escarpment into the plain in order to enclose the spring (Figures 4.9, 4.13). In spite of good defense, the Middle Bronze age city of Jericho was violently destroyed by vengeful raids of Egyptians after revival of their empire under the 18th Dynasty in 3560 B.P. and the driving of semitic Hyksos people from Egypt to Canaan.

The nearly 150-year cultural hiatus at Jericho after its destruction in late Middle Bronze ended with resetting of the tel about 3400 B.P. by Late Bronze people. No appreciable cultural difference is recognized between Middle Bronze and Late Bronze inhabitants. This suggests that the latter were the same as the former, both being Canaanite people who migrated south from the Phoenician coast probably because of another cold wet subphase and resultant tough climatic conditions in the European–north Asiatic territories. As Middle Bronze tombs were reused by new residents, it is possible that they also adjusted parts of Middle Bronze defenses to serve as their town walls. No evidence was found for the building of new such structures.

The Late Bronze city in turn was conquered, destroyed, and deserted apparently by Asiatic seminomads from the east about 3300 B.P. near the end of 14th century B.C. These could have been the rebellious slaves who escaped from Egypt during the reign of Ramses II (Kenyon, 1979, p. 205) and may be the basis for oral tradition about invasion of Israelites from the east led by Joshua. No archaeological evidence has survived to corroborate the biblical account of the conquest of Jericho. The upper part of the Late Bronze layer could have disappeared partially at Jericho a result of heavy erosion after its desertion because an intensive wet subphase actually occurred between the Late Bronze and Iron ages. Such a climatic event could have initiated another vigorous wave of southward migration from Europe and north Asiatic prairies. In 1200 B.C. there seemed to have been a dramatic change in civilization of the eastern Mediterranean. In their final and greatest attack about 1191 B.C. (3200 B.P.) the Sea People came by land and sea and were thrown back by Pharaoh Ramses III, who allowed them to settle on the Palestinian and Syrian coasts (Kenyon, 1979, pp. 208–212; Neumann, 1993, p. 231).

Jericho remained unsettled for a few hundred years between its destruction near the end of Late Bronze until 10th century B.C. (30th century B.P.). A Judean settlement established during the 7th or 6th century B.C. and maintained until the exile to Babylonia in the early 5th century B.C. contributed no new or important information regarding regional climatic history.

Discrepancy between archaeological chronology and biblical description of the conquest of Jericho by Joshua warrants reevaluation. Although it is widely accepted that invasion by the Israelites under Joshua should have occurred near the end of 13th century B.C., about 3200 B.P. or during the transition from the Late Bronze into the Iron ages, archaeological evidence from Jericho and Ai suggests that this description may have dealt with events that really happened but at an earlier time.

Oral tradition as recorded in the Bible incorporated three events, the first two of which are best explained by geological reasoning, whereas the third is man-made. The first is the crossing of the Jordan River (Joshua 3:13-16) that involved temporary cessation of flow of the river at the city of Adam (Figure 1.3; Bentor, 1989, pp. 327–28). That site is about 30 km north of the place east of Jericho (Fig. 2.14) where the Israelites crossed. From Adam (Damiya) Bridge (Figure 1.3) to a point about 20 km farther north incision by the river into the soft marly sequence of Lisan Formation left exceptionally high cliffs. The lower terrace is about 80 m below the upper terrace (Zor versus Ghor; Figures 2.13, 4.5, 4.6). In places this drop in level is within a distance of less than a half kilometer. Under these circumstances an earthquake could have caused the high cliffs at Adam to collapse, damming the river's course for a few days or hours.

The second event is destruction of the city wall so vividly described in Joshua 6:1–16. Although this event was attributed to divine intervention incorporating an acoustic resonance effect, a second earthquake or aftershock following the one that dammed the river should not be ignored as its cause. Rejuvenation of the Tel Jericho East fault (Figs. 4.8, 4.9) also could be associated. Evidences of repeated earthquakes that destroyed defense walls were found within excavated Early Bronze age layers (Kenyon, 1979, p. 92; Garstang, as quoted by Keller, 1957, p. 156).

The third event was the thorough burning of Jericho (Joshua 6:24) following the breakthrough of Israelites into the city. Archaeological evidences for similar burnings there during or just after invasions were found at the ends of both Early Bronze and Middle Bronze ages, although not at the end of the Late Bronze (Kenyon, 1979, p. 208). It is not unexpected that man-made destructions, including burning during conquests, would follow severe earthquakes. Social stresses could be induced by combined effects of earthquakes and climatic changes.

Droughts and famines often caused invasions by nomadic people driven from their places into neighboring more fertile and temperate areas. Raids and conquest from the east were a constant threat to Israel. Such fears were especially justified during times of administrative confusion following natural disasters. A good example of avoidance of these problems was provided by King Herod who rushed to Jericho to encourage and alert his troops there following a terrible earthquake in Judea and the Jordan Valley during the eighth year of his reign (Williamson, 1959). By that time, 31 B.C., neighboring nomads had already begun an invasion, believing that destruction and chaos resulting from the earthquake were so severe that conquest of Judea would be easy. Herod's firm measure was based on cumulative experience.

It is challenging on the basis of available archaeological data to select which of the three successive destructive events in Jericho during the three Bronze ages best fits the biblical description. Meager data left from the Late Bronze city does not enable us to decipher and reconstruct the way its civilization came to its end. Probably more evidence for that destruction once existed but largely disappeared during heavy erosion that followed. The few archaeological remains suggest that the city was not so important and well fortified as implied from description in the Book of Joshua. Moreover the time span of that particular city was less than 100 years—considerably shorter than the succession of Early Bronze cities, close to 1,000 years and that of Middle Bronze, 400 years. Middle Bronze walls were almost immune to earthquake collapse because of stability provided by their earth ramps. Violent destruction at the end of the Middle Bronze (1567 B.C.) was linked with the similar demise of many other important city-states in Canaan, all related to punitive campaigns by Egyptians after the driving back of the Hyksos (Kenyon, 1979, p. 177).

Archaeological evidence for the Early Bronze city indicates that the walls of Early Bronze III Jericho collapsed in a violent earthquake followed by man-caused burning. As oral traditions are unreliable about chronology (Kenyon, 1979, p. 205), this date best fits the prerequisites. Conceivably the Jericho seismic event happened by the end of Early Bronze III at the same time as the destruction of Sodom and Gomorrah in 4350 B.P. Both events were associated with very destructive earthquakes as well as with migrations. Both areas at opposite ends of the Dead Sea may have been destroyed by the same earthquake and that event may have been transplanted by oral tradition from Sodom and Gomorrah into a later conquest of Jericho by Joshua. This breakthrough into the Promised Land was another crucial event in the history of Israel as a rising nation, justifying the transferring of dramatic-divine actions into a later time.

The account of the capture of Ai by Joshua after the fall of Jericho (Joshua 7:7–8) is another example of a discrepancy between biblical description and archaeological chronology (Kenyon, 1979, p. 100–102). Excavations revealed that after several destructive events the fortified city of Ai was abandoned at the end of Early Bronze, about 4400 B.P., and was not reoccupied until later in the Iron age. These conclusions agree with the suggestion of Alt (1989) from the El Amarna letters of Egypt that the Israelite settling process in Canaan was the result of gradual immigration more than a century before the estimated date of the Israelite conquest and not because of a unified military campaign (Silberman, 1992).

Other interpretations for the settling process of Israelites in Canaan between the Middle Bronze and Iron ages based on paleodemographic and anthropologic criteria were developed by Finkelstein (1990) and Zertal (1990) in their studies of the hill country of Manasseh and the land of Ephraim. Zertal concluded that the process was a gradual one lasting from the Late Bronze through the Iron age. It proceeded from the desert fringe of Jordan into the interior valleys of Canaan and from there to the south and west foothills. Finkelstein (1990) considered that this process was linked with a demographic revolution in the hill country of Canaan beginning sometime in Middle Bronze. By that time people who later became Israelites were an integral part of the Canaanite population. No massive emigration from elsewhere would be required to explain the sudden establishment of Israelite settlements. "Sometime shortly after 1250 B.C., far to the west in the Aegean, a combination of political, climatic and economic factors brought an end to the power of the Mycenaean kingdoms, and this dramatic collapse disturbed the delicate balance of economic and political power in the entire eastern Mediterranean world" (Silberman, 1992, p. 30). A similar sequence also occurred in north Mesopotamia (Weiss et al., 1993).

The main contribution of archaeological data from Jericho is twofold: cultural history since Mesolithic time, about 11,000 B.P., and numerous breaks in its habitation. Both natural and man-made interruptions often are interrelated and may be results of climatic changes.

Bashan (South Syria) Volcanic Field

Supportive evidence for wetter than present climatic conditions near the break between the Early Bronze and Middle Bronze ages was provided by a unique find at Khirbet el Umbachi in south Syria (Figure 1.2, near Latitude 33°N, Longitude 37°E) about 130 km east of the Sea of Galilee (Dubertret and Dunand, 1954–55). About 40,000 skeletons of grass-eating mammals were found blanketed by lava flows (Figure 4.14). These were hunted and slaughtered by late Early Bronze people, as indicated by pottery sherds associated with the animals as well as by radiocarbon ages ranging between 4160 and 4075 B.P. from organic matter extracted from bones by heat of the lava. That basalt flow should

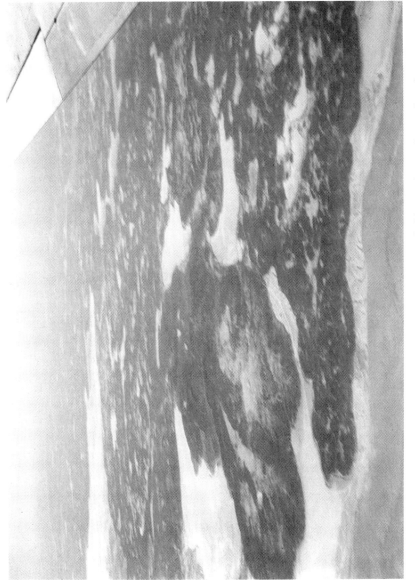

Figure 4.14. Lava flows in Jordan photographed in 1948. Probably similar to those of Bashan.

be younger than the volcanic cones, perhaps already within Climatic Wet Phase III, 3900 B.P. or later. Wetter than present climatic conditions were needed to feed such a large population of grass eaters. The strong bulls and well-fed cows of Bashan also are mentioned in Psalms 22:10–13 and Amos 4:1.

Blanketing basalt flows at Khirbet el Umbachi suggest renewal of volcanic activity near the end of Early Bronze over the entire Bashan volcanic province of Jebel Druze-Wadi Sirhan along a northwest-trending tensional feature. This activity may have been part of a global tectonic phase with explosive types of volcanism as an important component, leading to a genetic relationship with Climatic Wet Phase III. Climatic changes into wetter conditions can occur because of shielding by volcanic dust veils, especially if the latter are high enough to reach into the lower stratosphere. Under such circumstances, wet climatic phases may last appreciably longer than volcanic action. For example, a 150-year worldwide wave of exceptional activity is suggested by Lamb (1971) to have existed between A.D. 1750 and A.D. 1900. A 220-year rise of the Dead Sea level may have occurred between these same dates (Klein, 1986, chrono sheet no. 9). These data suggest that the wet climatic period may have lasted 30% longer than the source volcanic action even though they began at the same time.

Cumulative climatic effects from longer than usual epochs of volcanic activity could have lasted for periods ranging from centuries to tens of thousands of years (Fuchs, 1947; Lamb, 1971). The duration, intensity, and distribution patterns of volcanic eruptions and cold periods in turn may be related to magnitudes of tectonic movements attributed to convection within the earth's mantle. Indications for genetic relationship between tectonic phases and wet climatic conditions during the Holocene also were identified along the coastal plain of Israel (Neev, Bakler, and Emery, 1987). One example led to the break between Early Bronze and Middle Bronze and another was between Middle Bronze and Late Bronze.

Agricultural Soils and Fresh Waters in the Plain of Sodom

Availability of suitable soil and fresh water would have been key factors for settling and flourishing of large farming communities along fringes of the Dead Sea since Mid-Holocene. High porosity and permeability increase suitability of soils for agricultural usage by improving aeration of root systems, increasing mobility of supplies of nutrients for plants, and diminishing accumulation of harmful salts through better drainage of irrigated areas. These prerequisites are best met in sandy soils. In contrast, some clay is needed to enable absorption of water and nutrients. Validity of these criteria is demonstrated by excellent crops of vegetables grown at present just north of Mount Sedom where silty and sandy soils of the Zohar delta (Figure 4.15) were exposed during the post-1956 regression of the sea. This production occurs in spite of availability of only brackish water (Cl = 1,800 ppm) for irrigation with no indication of harmful accumulation of salts.

Similar soils now are being formed as lenses in other deltaic envi-

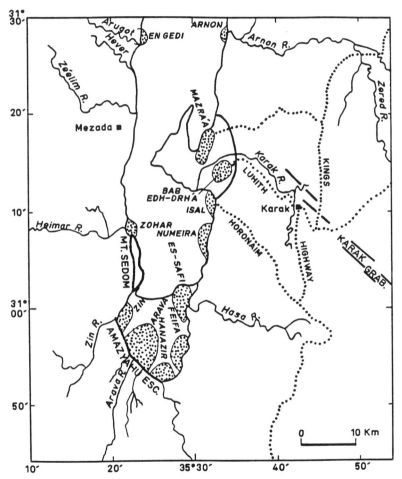

Figure 4.15. Map of the Dead Sea's south half from En Gedi and Arnon River in the north to Amazyahu fault escarpment in the south; dotted areas are alluvial fans at the mouths of rivers as potential sites for agricultural communities. Dotted lines are ancient routes leading from Jordanian plateau down to the Dead Sea and connecting routes to Judea, Egypt, and Elath. The unique location of the three main routes between Moab and Judea crossed the natural barrier of the East border fault escarpment through the biblical site of Zoar (Bab edh-Dhr'a), making its description as the latch (or key) to Moab a justified analogy. Heavy civilian and military transportation kept these three routes busy, especially the central one (Luhith).

ronments. The nearer the areas are to outlets of rivers from mountains, the higher their content of coarse grains. Streams coming from the south, mainly through Arava Valley, contribute more to accumulation of sandy soils than do most from mountains on the east and west. Floodwaters of the former are more heavily loaded with suspended sediments, much of which consists of quartz sand grains (Figure 4.15; Dan, 1981). Consequently suitable soils within alluvial fans along the belt at the foot of Amazyahu fault escarpment should be more widespread than in deltas along east and west escarpments.

At present more perennial rivers and springs flow into the Dead Sea from north and east than from south and west but even now there is potable water at numerous springs and shallow subsurface reservoirs along the foot of Amazyahu escarpment (Figures 1.4, 4.15). A more balanced situation may have existed in the past when more water was actively seeping into the sea. There are numerous ancient remains of now abandoned water installations, such as sugar mills and aqueducts, at spring sites used during Roman to Early Moslem times near the villages of Es-Safi and Mazra'a, mostly along the East border fault.

A similar change also may have happened along the foot of Amazyahu escarpment as the springs there are fed by seepages from reservoirs recharged by rains falling on the Judean, Negev, Moab, and Edom mountains (Figure 1.2) draining toward the Dead Sea, mostly as subsurface flows. Clearly the overall discharge of fresh and brackish waters from the mountains and Arava reservoirs into the south basin was reduced after Early Holocene. Lesser discharge could have existed twice during the Holocene especially after the wet phases of Pre-Pottery Neolithic B and the Middle to Late Bronze ages. Such depletion of reservoirs should have been long and gradual, lagging behind variations produced by year-to-year fluctuations of rainfall and seasonal runoff over catchment areas. These would have had an immediate response on levels of intermediate lakes as well as on those of the terminal sea. Effects of rejuvenated faulting along the south basin's border on the rate of freshwater seepages from springs could have been either negative or positive.

Probably availability of agricultural soils in the south basin is a more critical factor than freshwater for survival of agricultural communities. Longer-range depletion processes within subsurface reservoirs have a moderating influence on short-range climatic changes. Reasonable quantities of fresh to brackish water should continue flowing into the Sodom Plain even during dry periods so that irrigation farming can be maintained. A rise in sea level to near −300 m m.s.l. definitely would reduce or eliminate farming to the stage of abandonment of agricultural communities because freshwater is useless when suitable soils are submerged. Joint effects of tectonic subsidence of the bottom of the south basin and excessive supply of detrital sediments to its south fringe through the Arava and Zin rivers could be responsible for the burial and destruction of settlements and water installations, especially those from the Early Bronze age.

Climatic Fluctuations since 20,000 B.P. with Analogies from Adjacent Regions

Pleistocene

Variation of the heavy oxygen isotope ($\partial^{18}O$) contents in pelagic (swimming or floating) foraminiferal tests from ocean bottom sites enabled Imbrie et al. (1984) to identify numerous climatic events of the past 800,000 years. Their table 6 and figures 7 and 8 describe a sequence of alternating isotope enrichment (plus signs in the extreme values column of Table 3.2) and impoverishment (minus signs in Table 3.2). More than 20 stages reflect changes in the global volume of glacial ice and the presence of glacial and interglacial epochs. The four latest alternating cold and warm climatic stages listed indicate simultaneous climatic changes in the Dead Sea region and in open oceans. Data for the region are from Figures 3.1, 3.2, 3.5, 3.6 and from Kaufman et al. (1992).

Early and Mid-Pleistocene climatic stages cited by Imbrie et al. may correlate with those in the Dead Sea region, although most older data for the sea are concealed in the subbottom. An age of 350,000 B.P. by the $^{230}Th/^{234}U$ method was determined by Kaufman et al. (1992, fig. 5) for oolitic limestone, a Samra facies at an elevation of –190 m m.s.l. near Hazeva (Figure 1.3). This date suggests that outcrops of Samra Formation at 183,000 B.P. and an older 350,000 B.P. rock unit of similar limestone along fringes of the basin are separated by a hiatus. Additional older hiatuses probably are present within the Dead Sea Group. Formations missing in outcrops are mostly rocksalts sandwiched between marly sediments deposited from dilute brines of high-level lakes. Both types of sediments are buried in deeper parts of the basin and wedge out up-dip toward the critical level of –400 m m.s.l.

Details of cycles of alternating rocksalt and marl deposited during the younger half of Würm glacial stage (stages 2–4 of Imbrie et al., 1984; in Table 3.2 and Pleistocene climatic phases 5 to 8 in Figures 3.1, 3.2, 3.5, 3.6) indicate strong climatic fluctuations within that time span. During this major global glacial-pluvial stage the level of Lisan Lake was lowered several times from about –200 m m.s.l. to a depth below –400 m m.s.l. and rocksalt beds were deposited; then the lake rose again to its high levels.

An interglacial stage, 12,500 B.P. to the present, represented by the Dead Sea Formation correlates with stage 1 (Table 3.2). High levels of Lisan Lake, predecessor of the Dead Sea, prevailed during Late Pleistocene Würm glacial stage, 70,000 to 12,500 B.P. and are represented by the Lisan Formation that correlates with glacial stage 2–4 of Imbrie et al. The interglacial stage between the Würm and Riss stages of Lisan and Samra lakes, 128,000 to 70,000 B.P., is indicated by low levels of a relict water body. It is denoted by a yet unnamed rocksalt formation (Figures 2.10, 3.1) deposited during stage 5. The high level reached by Samra Lake is indicated by oolitic limestone of the Samra Formation and correlates with glacial stage 6 of Imbrie et al. (1984) between 183,000 and 128,000 B.P. This sequence of four Late Pleistocene climatic stages in the Dead Sea region agrees in general with the Alpine-European glacial stages including the Riss and Würm pluvials (Horowitz, 1979).

Correlation between the four climatic changes in the oceans and the Dead Sea during the Late Pleistocene is remarkable because samples were recovered from distant and different areas and environments. Oceanic samples are from the equatorial zone and the south hemisphere, whereas the Dead Sea samples are from midlatitudes of the north hemisphere. Different parameters used in analyses of samples from both areas indicate that these cyclic changes must have been global and simultaneous. It is reasonable to believe that these four relatively long climatic changes separated by several tens of thousands of years indicate a substantial global factor such as orbital variations cited by Milankovitch (1938)—obliquity, precession, and eccentricity of the earth's axis. Stratospheric volcanic dust veils may be another factor in these climatic changes, shielding much of the earth from solar radiation.

Holocene

The postglacial or interglacial time after the Pleistocene glacial epochs is known as the Holocene, during all or most of which Israel was occupied by people. During the latter half of this time, movements and conflicts between different groups of these people are the basis for much biblical history but without much explanation of climatic causes for these movements or conflicts. The following discussion describes climatic changes, mainly degrees of wet and dry, cold and hot, that are inferred from levels of the Dead Sea recorded from sediments and terraces, from plant fossils, and from interpretation of human activities. Dating of the changes is chiefly by radiometric methods guided by archaeological sequences. By such means the environments at the time of destruction of Sodom, Gomorrah, and Jericho can be viewed to some extent as the participants may have seen them.

Nine or ten wet climatic events occurred in the Dead Sea region during the four phases of the Holocene, although only eight are evident on the gamma-ray log (Figure 3.2; Tables 3.3, 3.4). In the latter, amplitudes and wave lengths of these events are smaller than intervals during the eight phases of the Lisan or Würm stage but much more prominent than those during Riss-Würm (Samra-Lisan) interglacial

(Figure 3.1). Altogether 16 cultural ages existed in the region during the Holocene since 12,500 B.P., separated from each other by distinct breaks. Ten of these ages correspond with wet climatic phases marked by asterisks in Table 3.4 that denote possible seismic and volcanic activities.

The climatic pattern of the Holocene in the eastern Mediterranean-Levant-Mesopotamia region that includes the Dead Sea parallels that of Europe and to a lesser extent that of North America (Neumann and Parpola, 1987). In contrast, the climatic pattern of the Sahel-Chad-Ethiopia zone of Africa displays a mirror-image or negative correlation with the Alpine–Dead Sea regions.

The simplest model that best explains such an inverse pattern involving a north-south shift of climatic belts is well demonstrated by similar patterns in north Africa during the past 20,000 years. During that time span wet subphases in the Maghreb, the Atlas Mountains of northwest Africa, correspond with arid climates in the south Sahara–east Ethiopia region (Rognon, 1987, figs. 2, 3; Gasse and Street, 1978, fig. 10). This mirror-image pattern in adjacent climatic belts was a secondary effect superimposed on global processes of cooling during glacial stages and warming in interglacials. These processes may be associated with such specific regional conditions as directions and distances to larger water bodies as documented by Gasse (1977, fig. 2). During glacial stages or substages of Late Pleistocene, the south Sahara–east Ethiopia zone was dominated both by hyperaridity and low temperatures, while at the same time wet cold conditions prevailed in the Europe–Dead Sea–Atlas region. During interglacials of Late Pleistocene and Holocene when levels of lakes in Ethiopia such as Lake Abh'e were high, climatic conditions there were defined as temperate-tropical and tropical, respectively.

An attempt was made (Figure 4.16) to compare climatic fluctuations in the Dead Sea region (Figure 3.6) with those in the south Sahara–east Ethiopia region of Africa as well as in Scandinavia (Gary et al., 1974) and the Alps in Europe (Bortenschlager, 1982). In light of uncertainties in radiocarbon dates, the suggested pattern is reasonable. The figure demonstrates a direct correlation between the Dead Sea and European zones and an inverse one with south Sahara–east Ethiopia.

The continuous line for north Europe summarizes the descriptions of the ten climatic intervals during the Holocene (Gary et al., 1974). The first of this sequence is a cold interval named Oldest Dryas that peaked at 13,000 B.P.—still within Pleistocene or the latest Würm glacial stage.

The sharpest and most prominent climatic break between Pleistocene and Holocene seems to have occurred in both Europe and the Dead Sea regions during transition between Climatic Phases I and II or from Boreal to Atlantic periods about 7,500 years ago. This differs from

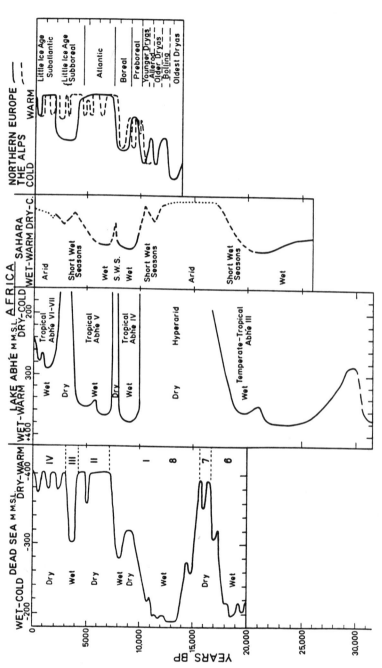

Figure 4.16. Comparison of climatic fluctuations during latest Pleistocene and Holocene in the Dead Sea region inferred from radiometric-dated levels relative to mean sea level of the ocean. Lake Abh'e (Gasse, 1977; Gasse and Street, 1978) in Ethiopia and Djibouti has undergone changes of level largely out of phase with those of the Dead Sea because of their latitudinal position (Latitude 11°N vs. 31°N). Climates of the south Sahara (Rognon, 1987) also are partly out of phase, probably for the same reason. In contrast, climates of Europe (Gary, McAfee and Wolf, 1974; Bortenschlager, 1982) based on temperature changes determined from extent of ice cover are more nearly synchronous with those of the region.

an earlier interpretation (Neev and Emery, 1967) of a complete desiccation of the Dead Sea about 10,000 B.P. related to the retreat of European glaciers and shrinkage of Lisan Lake.

Data from different sources indicate that chronologies of Climatic
Phase II in Europe, the Levant, and Ethiopia-Sahara in Africa are similar to each other. The dryest as well as the warmest postglacial climate
prevailed in Europe as in many other regions during the Atlantic Interval about 7500 to 4500 B.P. (Gary et al., 1974). Three wet subphases,
each 200 to 300 years long, occurred in the Alps during the Chalcolithic
and Early Bronze ages or Climatic Phase II. The first was about 6,000
years ago and the other two just before and after 5000 B.P. (Bortenschlager, 1982). A time span of 4,000 years—7500 to 3500 B.P.—was
determined for cave drawings found in the Tassilie Ahaggar hills of the
south Algeria Sahara. These drawings reflect the presence of a rich
tropical-wet mammal assemblage as well as human communities in that
region, which is now bone-dry (Muzzolini, 1992). An inverse wet-dry
relationship between the Sahara and the middle latitude region of the
Mideast and Europe is corroborated (Figure 4.16).

The cold Climatic Wet Phase III also prevailed in Europe where it
was described as a subboreal interval that followed the Atlantic one from
about 4500 to 2500 B.P. It was defined as very cold, approaching frigid-
ity (Gary et al., 1974, p. 705). Data available indicate that apparently it
lasted about 700 years. During the same time inverse climatic conditions of a dry cold phase existed in the south Sahara–east Ethiopia zone
of Africa.

Perhaps an explanation for the negative correlation pattern in the
south Sahara–east Ethiopia and Dead Sea–Alpine zones could be found
in secondary processes as sudden injections of large volumes of melt-
water into the North Atlantic Ocean. A blanket of light water may have
shut off production of the ocean's deep waters. Another product of that
process could be reduction of northward heat transport in the Atlantic
so that warmer than average water was generated south of the equator
(Street-Perrott and Perrott, 1990). Persistent asymmetrical surface temperature patterns in the Atlantic could generate simultaneously the sudden cold weather episodes in Europe as Younger Dryas 11,000 to 10,000
years ago during which ". . . a return to almost fully glacial conditions
occurred" (Berger and Labeyrie, 1987, p. 13) and abrupt droughts in
the sub-Sahara belt of Africa. Interpretation of climatic events may be
hampered by miscorrelations caused by technical problems, such as un-
explained anomalous results of radiocarbon dating.

Gasse and Street (1978, p. 316) stated that for the Ethiopia rift and
Afar region, "Early and mid-Holocene were times of very high water
levels. All lakes transgressed rapidly after 11,000 to 10,000 B.P., reaching maximum elevations towards 9400 B.P. They retreated very mark-
edly towards 4000 B.P." A similar sequence of events with some age

differences is presented by Servant and Servant-Vildary (1980, figs. 6.6, 6.8, 6.9) for climatic fluctuations within the Chad basin during Early and Mid-Holocene supporting an inverse correlation with the curve of Dead Sea levels (Figure 4.16).

Transition from the latest pluvial phase of Würm into Holocene is ill-defined. On the composite log (Fig. 3.2) it is expressed as a 5-m marl layer deposited in the south basin during a period of 7,200 years between the beginning of the Geometric Kebaran age from 15,000 B.P. and the end of Pre-Pottery Neolithic B in 7800 B.P. On the gamma-ray log this marl layer is shown as a prominent and massive positive anomaly with a few superimposed humps. Average climatic conditions in the region during that time span are described as a wet cold phase. Variation of arboral pollen in sediments deposited during the same time span farther north in the graben (A. Horowitz, 1992, p. 417) and chronology of cultural changes at different sites (Bar-Yosef, 1987) yielded a more detailed subdivision of regional distinction of paleoclimatic conditions as follows: Geometric Kebaran together with Early Natufian (15,000–12,500 B.P.)— wet cold; Late Natufian (11,000–10,500 B.P.)—dry cold; Pre-Pottery Neolithic A and B (10,300–7800 B.P.)—wet cold. Exact correlation of this climatic subdivision could not be made with specific lithologic or gamma-ray intensity changes. It is probably better to earmark the lower half of that marl unit as the eighth climatic phase of Late Pleistocene and the upper half as the first phase of Holocene with some overlapping.

A. Horowitz (1979, p. 343) correlated the time interval of 11,000 to 7000 B.P. or Climatic Phase I with European Versilian substage and referred to its climate as an interpluvial "corresponding more or less to that of the present, with only minor fluctuations." He also pointed out that during this interval global sea level probably rose 2 or 3 m above the present level. He made no reference to possible effects of subsequent cumulative tectonic uplifts of the land along the Israeli coast (Neev et al., 1987). According to Gary et al. (1974) the climate of Boreal Interval from 9000 to 7000 B.P. was relatively wetter and cooler than the following Atlantic Interval (Figure 4.16). It is surprising that Wet Subphase I-a during Pre-Pottery Neolithic B was not noticed in Europe (Berger and Labeyrie, 1987). Perhaps future studies and more precise dating techniques may indicate that Younger Dryas correlates with that wet subphase.

Climatic Phase II occurred during Middle Holocene extending nearly 3,900 years between 7800 and 3900 B.P. and including the Late Neolithic, Chalcolithic, and Early Bronze ages. It was dominated by dry climate as indicated by abundant rocksalt deposition in the Dead Sea south basin but was interrupted by Wet Subphase II-a at about 6300 B.P. and Wet Subphase II-b between 4900 and 4600 B.P. The implied long dry climatic regime of Mid-Holocene in the region (Phase II) parallels the description of the Atlantic Interval of Europe from 7500 to 4500 B.P. (Gary et al., 1974; Bortenschlager, 1982) except for a few hundred years discrepancy in dating. Their definition of the Atlantic Interval differs from those of A. Horowitz (1979, p. 343) who related pluvial climatic conditions to the Atlantic substage in Israel and to simultaneous regression of the Mediterranean Sea caused by a drop of the world's ocean level by 5 or 6 m below present.

The 700-year long Climatic Wet Phase III began about 3900 B.P. in Middle Bronze II and ended about 3200 B.P. at the close of the Late Bronze age. It was preceded by the Intermediate Bronze age which had several dramatic events that made it unique. First were the very destructive earthquakes at Sodom and Gomorrah and perhaps also at Jericho by the end of Early Bronze III about 4350 B.P. after the long period of tectonic quiescence during Climatic Phase II. These earthquakes marked a gradual transition from the moderate climate of Early Bronze into drier conditions toward 4200 B.P. Seismic events together with the moderate climatic warming process initiated extensive invasion of nomadic people from the east and northeast deserts into Canaan. These invaders conquered and settled many sites with no chronological hiatus.

Abrupt climatic change expressed by appreciable worsening of the drought occurred during the second half of Intermediate Bronze between 4200 and 3900 B.P. Results were more devastating than man-made changes during military occupation and produced the longest and most overwhelming cultural break recorded in Canaan and neighboring countries involving massive desertion and dwindling of Canaan's population (Kochavi, 1967; Kenyon, 1979; R. Amiran and Kochavi, 1985; Gophna, 1992).

Marked increase in aridity occurred abruptly also in north Mesopotamia at 4200 B.P. when extensive dry farming territories were deserted by local inhabitants who migrated toward south Mesopotamia, generating an economic disintegration process that led to collapse of the Akkadian Empire (Weiss et al., 1993). This period of drought and cultural hiatus lasted for 300 years ending at 3900 B.P. when climatic conditions ameliorated. Deserted areas then were reoccupied under the rule of an emerging Amorite or Amurru regime. This sequence of events agrees with climatic chronology for the Dead Sea region at exactly the same time. Weiss et al. identified three earlier periods of drought at 7900, 6500, and 5000 B.P. based on similar cultural-sedimentological evidence in north Mesopotamia.

An intensive resettling process then occurred in Canaan at some time between 4000 and 3800 B.P. with the beginning of Climatic Wet Phase III. Invading new settlers were west Asiatic-Semitic people who brought with them highly developed cultural traditions. The best explanation for such a massive migration could be a progression when colder conditions in north and central Asiatic Siberian prairies and

Alpine-Carpathian-Caucasian mountain ranges drove people from areas where they could not survive into territories farther south with warmer climates. Pressures laid by these refugees on Anatolian and south European peoples pushed the latter then to emigrate from their homes and settle in the dry farming lands of Canaan that were almost vacant after the heavy drought of the Intermediate Bronze age. Middle Bronze II people who came from the north had no problems in settling Canaan, first along the coastal belt, then gradually moving inland from the Mediterranean Sea.

Cultural similarity of Late Bronze to Middle Bronze people in Canaan explains the absence of a real demographic break between them. Santorini or Thera volcanic eruptions in about 3620 B.P. or during the later part of the Middle Bronze age lead to the suggestion that Climatic Wet Phase III extended from Middle Bronze into Late Bronze. An intensive erosional event at Jericho near the end of Late Bronze suggests that the last episode of Climatic Wet Phase III separated the Late Bronze age from the Iron ages. Symmetric configuration on the gamma-ray curve indicates three consecutive episodes (Figure 3.2), a main peak at its middle and secondary peaks before and after it. The main peak could have been sometime within the Middle Bronze age, perhaps associated with the Santorini eruption, whereas the two secondary subphases were about 3900 and 3200 B.P., respectively.

Most aspects of this interpretation are corroborated by data on climatic changes in Europe and the Mideast during 4th millennium B.P. Modern studies of glacial variations and tree-ring densities within the subalpine zone indicate that climate during most of the Middle and Late Bronze ages had two subphases of cold weather, 3800 to 3470 B.P. and 3400 to about 3230 B.P., separated by a short warm interval. The second cold subphase came abruptly and ". . . is considered to have been the coldest and longest sustained cold period of the past 8000 years, colder than the recent Little Ice Age of the CE (ed. Common Era)" (Neumann, 1993, p. 231). An intensive migration occurred during the 13th and the beginning of the 12th centuries B.C., 3300 to 3150 B.P. These people moved by land and sea from central and southeast Europe toward the Mideast, reaching as far as the Nile delta. Their desperate attempt to gain a bridgehead in Egypt (Kenyon, 1979, p. 212) indicates that severity of climatic change in their homelands drove them into that adventure. Surprisingly no evidence was found for a similar large-scale wave of migration for people in southeast Europe at the beginning of Middle Bronze II, 3900 to 3800 B.P. Volcanic eruptions on a global scale that maintained a long-lasting dust veil probably caused the long duration and wide distribution of Climatic Wet Phase III.

Late Holocene or Climatic Phase IV in the Dead Sea region lasted from 3200 B.P. to the present, following Climatic Wet Phase III at the end of the Late Bronze age. It had frequent alternations of dry and wet subphases of moderate amplitudes and relatively short wave lengths. Three of them are considered main wet subphases according to the gamma-ray log (Figures 3.2, 3.6) and data from the Mount Sedom caves (Frumkin et al., 1991).

Wet Subphase IV-a is surmised to have occurred during the time range of Assyrian-Babylonian-Persian-Hellenistic conquests of Israel and Judea or between 2700 and 2300 B.P. This estimate is derived from data of glacier advances, snowlines in the Alps, and tree-ring densities (Neumann, 1992, table 1). Dates of ancient barley harvest during the Neo-Babylonian culture in Mesopotamia indicated to Neumann and Sigrist (1978) that the time between 2800 and 2400 B.P. was cool and wet. Their literature survey suggests that this 400-year period was the peak of an even longer regime of more rainfall and moister conditions than now. It extended between 2850 and 2200 B.P. until Roman times and affected middle latitudes of the north hemisphere between North America and Europe.

Wet Subphase IV-b correlates with west and south invasions of Huns, Slavs, and Goths from north Europe and Asia and the collapse of the Roman Empire, all prior to 1500 B.P. During both Wet Subphases IV-a and IV-b, the level of the Dead Sea rose to –375 m m.s.l. (Table 3.3; Figure 3.6). Wet Subphase IV-c could have been during late Crusader and early Mamluk times, about 850 to 750 B.P., as indicated by tree-ring density studies of *Juniperus phoenica* that grew in the nearby Negev mountains (Waisal and Liphschitz, 1968). Wet Subphase IV-d may correlate either with the Little Ice Age of A.D. 1550 (440 B.P.), with that of A.D. 1830 to 1930 (160 to 60 B.P.), or with both during rule of the Turks in the Mideast.

Wet Subphase II-b was probably during the Early Bronze II age, 4900 to 4650 B.P. (Table 3.3), whereas Wet Subphase II-a could have happened sometime in Chalcolithic about 6500 to 6000 B.P. The latter dates are near enough to the time of the epic flood described in *Gilgamesh* (Gardner and Maier, 1984), first assembled and pressed in cuneiform characters on twelve tablets about 5200 B.P. The Babylonian Utnapishtim, Gilgamesh's ancestor, was instructed by Ea, Sumerian Enki or Lord of the Earth, to build a ship and load it with the seed of all living things, cattle, beasts, and his family. According to the story, the ship survived the flood about 6000 B.P. and landed on Mount Nisir. This account must have been current at Uruk, the religious capital where Gilgamesh was king and known to Abraham who lived at Ur—now Eridu—only 60 km distant until he emigrated to Canaan. Evidently the story of Utnapishtim's flood evolved into the later and more detailed story of Noah's Flood. Probably this story of Noah was carried to Canaan as a derivation from the earlier record as could be implied from close similarities in the two accounts (Keller, 1957, pp. 35–39). The possible date of the Gilgamesh-Utnapishtim flood may correspond with the beginning of

Wet Subphase II-a but that story itself could have been handed down from similar but older events through oral traditions (Gardner and Maier, 1984). Possibly heavy rains that began about 3900 B.P. during Climatic Phase III (Table 3.3) revived interest in the older story, later leading to the saga of Noah's Flood, purportedly happening in 4300 B.P. under a different religion. In the same manner, earthquakes that destroyed Sodom and Gomorrah may have led to the concept of destruction of Jericho by divine intervention.

Many indications of past large-scale changes in the Dead Sea level can be useful for learning about these related flood epics. No evidence has been found for a world-encircling flood during the Holocene either from sea levels high enough to fill the graben and leave high shorelines or from marked dilution of brines recorded in sediments from oceanic water deposited on the floor of the sea. The existing information merely implies an approximate 3900 B.P. beginning of a 700- to 800-year wet climatic period as indicated by higher levels. There is no recognized evidence for dilution of brine in the graben that would be expected if large enough volumes of water were added to the ocean to allow Utnapishtim's ship to be stranded on Mount Nisir, perhaps 2,700 m above sea level, or later for Noah's Ark on Mount Ararat (5,137 m) or its flank. Each probably was the highest mountain that then was known to inhabitants of the low flat Tigris-Euphrates Valley.

Absence of evidence within sediments means that these floods, no matter how enormous, were not high enough to have to have raised ocean level sufficiently to submerge the sills that separate the Dead Sea depression from the ocean so that flow could pass through the Jezreel or Arava Valleys to the Dead Sea graben. Both stories appear to be overstatements by populations who lived on broad lowlands or reflections of experiences of still more ancient peoples who may have lived during Late Pleistocene times of rapidly rising sea levels caused by melting of glaciers. Confirmation of the absence of a world-encircling flood during Late Holocene is provided by studies of sediments in other lakes of the earth—for example, a coastal lake of Late Pleistocene glacial origin in Massachusetts in the United States, where flora, fauna, and $\partial^{13}C$ and $\partial^{18}O$ show no changes that could have been expected from intrusion of seawater at the biblical date of Noah's Flood (Emery, 1969).

5

Coordination of Biblical and Scientific Information

General

Much knowledge of biblical events is from narratives of ancient oral tradition that justify analysis and respect because they may reflect genuine and unique historical information. The problems involved with such study are demonstrated by descriptions of three different events related in the stories of Sodom and Gomorrah, Jericho, and the narrative of Noah's Flood. All three are associated with two processes: geologic-tectonic activity of vast areas with resulting submergence of soils or destruction of settlements. The first two tell about tectonism within the Dead Sea region at south basin and Jericho where many sites are identifiable. The Sodom and Gomorrah event could have happened only at the end of Early Bronze III, as implied from archaeological chronology and outline of the biblical story. The same could be true also for Jericho if not for a significant difference in chronology of the two stories.

Expulsion of rebellious Asiatic tribes from Egypt is recorded in Egyptian history to have taken place during the 13th century B.C. At least some of these seminomadic ex-slaves reportedly invaded Canaan from the east near the end of the Late Bronze age (Kenyon, 1979, pp. 205, 210) and conquered Hazor and other cities. No archaeological data were found to indicate the existence of defense walls or of a large densely populated city at Jericho during Late Bronze so the question of conquest remains open. Invasions by nomadic tribes from the east and conquests of Jericho had occurred earlier—for example, 1,000 years prior to the end of Early Bronze III (Kenyon, 1979, p. 91). Evidence for collapse of Jericho's defense walls during earthquakes and for fires during conquests in late Early Bronze III were found by archaeologists. The importance of the capture of Jericho after the Exodus was so great for Judaic history that the story may have been enhanced by inclusion of information from earlier oral traditions of the Sodom and Gomorrah earthquake. New studies are augmenting previous knowledge of the development of Israelites as a nation and the effect of increased numbers of descendants of nomadic tribes who fled from Egypt to Canaan (Finkelstein, 1990; Zertal, 1990; Silberman, 1992).

There is no evident connection of Noah's Flood with Canaan or more specifically with the Dead Sea region. Although unusually extensive flooding of dry lake plains within the Jordan and Dead Sea valleys often occurred during Holocene, none could have been as great as the biblical Noah's Flood when no land reportedly could be seen from the Ark. The width of the Jordan–Dead Sea graben is not more than 17 km and it is bordered on both sides by mountain ranges higher than 1,000 m.

A closer relation may exist between that story and the relict of a Hurrian version of the Gilgamesh epic from the beginning of 2nd millennium B.C. found in a recently excavated royal Hittite archive. The hero's name in that younger version is not Utnapishtim but Nahamoliel, which is phonetically close to Noah as referred to in Genesis 5:29, "This name shall comfort us," or in Hebrew '*Ze Yenahamennu*' (Encyclopedia Hebraica, 1955, 10:776–78). Clearly the biblical flood event could have been derived from the earlier Sumerian-Hurrian-Babylonian epics.

Interpretion of the Sodom and Gomorrah saga was based on comparison of the biblical description of the event with available geological, climatological, and archaeological knowledge of the region. The hard core of the physical aspects of that event is concisely expressed by a few verses in Genesis 19:24–28: "The LORD rained upon Sodom and Gomorrah brimstone and fire from the LORD out of heaven; and He overthrew those cities and all the plain, and all the inhabitants of the cities and all that grew upon the ground. But his (Lot's) wife looked back from behind him, and she became a pillar of salt. And Abraham got up early in the morning to the place where he stood before the LORD, and he looked toward Sodom and Gomorrah and toward all the land of the plain, beheld, and, lo, the smoke of the country went up, as the smoke of a furnace. And it came to pass, when God destroyed the cities of the plain that God remembered Abraham, and sent Lot out of the midst of the overthrow, when he overthrew the cities in which Lot dwelt." This quotation was chosen from the Torah, as edited by Stirling (1954), because it is the basis for the classic translation into the English Bible and is less interpretative than newer versions. For example, the Hebrew word that was translated as "overthrow" in this quotation is sometimes translated as "annihilated," but the former is more appropriate for the action of an earthquake. All other quotations in this text are from the Torah translation edited by Plant (1981).

The Arena

An important part of the background is the arena, the nature of the events, and locations of problematic though important sites in the Plain of Sodom (Figures 1.3, 1.4). The phrases "all the plain of the Jordan" in Genesis 13:10 and "all the plain" not mentioning the Jordan River in Genesis 19:25 differ somewhat from each other in their meaning. In this interpretation the phrase "all the plain of the Jordan" refers to the entire scope of the Dead Sea basin that extends along the rift valley from near the Yabboq or Zarqa River in the north to Amazyahu fault escarpment in the south. This phrase is used in the description of the separation of Abraham and Lot during which Lot observed the plain from a high topographic point above the Jordan Valley west of Jericho. The valley just beneath him was considered to be an integral part of "all the plain of the Jordan." The same verses indicate that the sites of Sodom, Gomorrah, and Zoar also were encompassed within the whole "plain of the Jordan" (Genesis 13:10–12).

Genesis 19:25 where the ending "of the Jordan" is missing refers only to the Dead Sea south basin because it deals with five cities, at least three of which were within that area. Sodom, associated phonetically with Mount Sedom (*Jebel Usdum*), borders the west flank of the south basin and must have been near the salt diapir. As Sodom and Gomorrah and perhaps the other cities of the plain except Zoar were totally destroyed during this event, it is reasonable to suppose that Sodom and Gomorrah also were within the south basin. Precise location of Zoar still is being argued, although it probably was east of the Lisan Peninsula close to the East border fault (Albright, Kalso, and Palin, 1944; Neev and Emery, 1967). These three cities probably were within the south basin. The other two of the five cities of the plain, Admah and Zeboiim, also could have been within the south basin or the Plain of Sodom, although they are not mentioned by name in the context of the destruction.

The term "all the plain of the Jordan" thus includes four segments (Figures 1.2, 1.3): the lower Jordan Valley between the Yabboq River and the Dead Sea, the north basin, Lisan Peninsula, and the Plain of Sodom, which is the surface of the south basin (Neev and Emery, 1967; Figures 1.3, 1.4, 2.1, 2.2, 4.15). The south basin and north basin together with the Lisan Peninsula between them are three components of the Dead Sea graben. In ancient times during dry climatic phases, the deep water of the north basin separated the two emerged and fertile flats, on one side the lower Jordan Valley and on the other much of the south basin. Both basins have subsided almost continuously since they were formed, the north basin more than the south. Because of that the bottom of the north basin is the lowest structural and bathymetric part of the sea. It functioned as a terminal water body that accumulated deep residual brines probably ever since the Miocene Period; thus, the depositional plain of the north basin could never have been a site for agricultural communities.

Biblical description of total destruction of Sodom and Gomorrah (Genesis 19:25) refers specifically to the inner area or depressed part of the south basin, the Plain of Sodom with its uncompacted sediments and not to its flanks along border fault zones. Zoar, identified with Bab edh-Dhr'a, was situated on bedrock at the northeast flank of the south basin or east of the Lisan Peninsula and was not destroyed. The other four Early Bronze age tels along the East border fault, Numeira, Es-Safi, Feifa, and Hanazira (Figure 1.3), probably also survived as they occupy sites on bedrock.

Several documents of Byzantine through medieval and later times suggest that some of the five named cities of the plain could have been within the Dead Sea north basin and even farther west or north (as compiled by Braslavy, 1956, pp. 314–15). Van Seters (1975, as quoted by Rast, 1987) noted his acceptance of a north location for Admah and Zeboiim and a south one for Sodom and Gomorrah. Rast (p. 191) did not rule out this possibility but stressed his view ". . . that the popular tradition of the Sodom and Gomorrah couplet sprang from the southeast end of the Dead Sea basin." Considering the steep slopes along both the East and West border faults and the fluctuating level of the water body, the north basin should have functioned as a physical obstacle that interfered with mutual economic, physical, social, and cultural contacts between inhabitants of the two fertile "plains" north and south of it. As the five cities of the plain often were mentioned as a unified group (Genesis 19:29) and as there was some kind of cooperation between them during wartime (Genesis 14), presumably all five were within the south basin.

Fruitful archaeological studies along the east flank of the south basin have been conducted since 1973 by Rast and Schaub following the pioneering efforts of Albright (1924), Glueck (1937), Albright et al. (1944), and Lapp (1968a, 1968b, 1970). Identification of five Early Bronze sites in the east part of the basin was reported by Rast and Schaub (1974, 1980, 1981) and Rast (1987, and personal communication, 1989). Although to date only Bab edh-Dhr'a and Numeira have been thoroughly excavated, three other sites, Es-Safi, Feifa, and Khanazir (Figures 1.3, 1.4, 4.15) also were settled during the Early Bronze age. All five sites are on elevated points along the hinge line of the south basin in the East border fault zone, suggesting a pattern dictated primarily by defensive considerations of Early Bronze people. Similar patterns also were practiced by people farther north on both sides of the Jordan Valley, although large unfortified sites existed during the same period in the central flat parts of basins such as Beth She'an. The economy of the settlements in the Sodom plain was essentially agricultural with grazing being secondary.

Bab edh-Dhr'a was occupied continuously between Early Bronze I and the end of Early Bronze IV, whereas Numeira was inhabited only during Early Bronze III (Table 3.3). By the end of this age, both Bab edh-Dhr'a and Numeira (Nimrin, Isaiah 15:6) had been severely damaged by two earthquakes. Numeira then was deserted but Bab edh-Dhr'a was resettled immediately, perhaps by invading seminomadic people of the Intermediate Bronze age, who took advantage of the confusion caused by the natural disaster.

Reconnaissance surveys by archaeologists who tried to find Early Bronze sites within the inner limit of the south basin and a short-term underwater archaeological survey in the Dead Sea (Baney, 1962) had negative results. Following these and positive results of their own excavations on land at the east fringe of the basin, Rast and Schaub do not expect additional Early Bronze settlements to be found within the subsiding part of the basin, including its south and west flanks. The possibility that remains of such sites could have disappeared because of geological processes—subsidence following earthquakes, submergence by the sea, and burial by sediments—was dismissed by Rast (1987, p. 193) as speculative theories devoid of archaeological or geological support. Rast also concluded (after Klein, 1961) that tectonic activity was minimal during historic times.

There is value in reconsidering these conclusions of Rast and Schaub. Although Early Bronze age sites (most of them fortified) were built along the east and west fringes of the Jordan Valley, this is not the total pattern. Early Bronze sites also are present along the trough of the valley within cultivated lands, apparently because of economic considerations and efficiency (Zori, 1962; Ben-Arieh, 1965). Some sites were subject to flooding during wet climatic conditions so there is no reason why Early Bronze settlements, perhaps more than five of them, would not have been built within subsiding parts of the south basin if suitable soils and water were available.

The results of archaeological exploration by both Albright et al. (1944) and Rast (1987) led them to suggest an association of the Sodom and Gomorrah tradition with Early Bronze III settlements in the south basin. Other sites of the same and younger ages could have existed within that basin. For example, several kinds of human activity could have occurred there during most of the Iron age (First Temple time). This is indicated both by biblical reports and by archaeological excavations along the west flanks of the basin, such as at Mezed Gozal at the northwest corner of Mount Sedom where an 11th-century B.C. fortress was discovered (Aharoni, 1964a) and at En Gedi where a 7th-century

B.C. settlement and a Chalcolithic site were found (Mazar et al., 1966). Other structures of the 8th century B.C. are along the northwest coast of the sea (Bar-Adon, 1977).

It may be questioned why so few Iron age sherds were found at Es-Safi, Feifa, and Khanazir (Figure 1.4) and why nothing of that age was traced at Bab edh-Dhr'a and Numeira (Rast and Schaub, 1974). Perhaps settlements of that time did exist but were closer to the trough of the basin and at lower elevations. Braslavy (1956, pp. 323, 380) considered that sites in the south basin could have shifted several times. They may have moved downslope during periods of low levels to be covered later by sediments of alluvial fans from torrential floods or were flooded during times of high sea level. The effects of these sedimentary processes could have been enhanced by tectonic subsidence. Lowering of freshwater levels in reservoirs due to differential vertical land movements and falling sea levels also could have contributed to a basinward shift of sites. Such processes are not unique but their magnitude and frequency are larger in a terminal body such as the Dead Sea than in intermediate lakes.

The main conclusions of Donahue's studies (1980, 1981, 1985) on the geology of Early Bronze sites at Bab edh-Dhr'a and Numeira refer to a seismic origin of the cultural break near the end of Early Bronze III and changing rates of tectonic activity across the East border fault zone during preoccupation, occupation, and postoccupation stages of the Early Bronze age. His conclusions come from evidence of sudden extensive collapse of strongly built structures at these sites and from changing rates of erosion near them. These studies developed a sequence of changes in degradational-aggradational regimes. During the first stage a mild degradational regime prevailed and morphologies were gentle with bowl-shaped gorges at both Wadi Karak and Wadi Numeira. Elevations of the wadi troughs were 20 to 30 m shallower than now. This stage is correlative probably with the Natufian to the Pre-Pottery Neolithic ages, including Wet Subphase I-a of Holocene during the first shrinkage of Lisan Lake.

The next stage was neither aggradational nor degradational. It started during the dry warm climate of the Chalcolithic or Late Pottery Neolithic age and continued throughout most of the Climatic Optimum, 7800 to 3900 B.P., when the rate of erosion had to be minimal and before the sites of Bab edh-Dhr'a and Numeira were occupied. This stage continued into the occupation during the Early and Intermediate Bronze ages (4200 to 3900 B.P.) when a wetter subphase occurred, although the overall climate remained dry. There are indications that about that time a freshwater spring lay within the city wall of Bab edh-Dhr'a. During the following postoccupational time, the degradational regime was renewed and erosion vigorously increased. Steep narrow canyons 30 to 50 m deep were entrenched along the troughs of Wadi Karak parallel to the north flank of Bab edh-Dhr'a and Wadi Numeira to the point of changing local drainage patterns (Donahue, 1985, fig. 3).

Donahue related this last change in nature and rate of erosion to a lowering of the Dead Sea by tens of meters through a differential vertical tectonic movement during and after Early Bronze IV or the Intermediate Bronze age near the East border fault escarpment. This agrees with the conclusion reached by Macumber and Head (1991) for the Wadi el Hammeh area across the fault system south of the Sea of Galilee and the Yarmuk River (Figures 1.2, 4.1). Even though rejuvenated vertical differential tectonic movements associated with earthquakes occurred during and after Early Bronze III to IV, evidence is not available to support vertical shifts that could have exceeded a few meters. Abnormally high rainfall of Climatic Wet Phase III in Middle to Late Bronze is preferred as the main cause of that degradational regime.

Locations of Key Sites within the Dead Sea Basin

General

Not all five Early Bronze sites found by Rast and Schaub (1978) along the east limit of the Dead Sea south basin should be related to the five cities of the plains. The latter probably existed elsewhere in the basin. Several implications should be drawn. Perhaps more Early Bronze cities than the five biblical ones existed simultaneously in the plain of Sodom. Their distribution pattern could have consisted of a few central larger cities surrounded by many smaller ones. This concept agrees with the expression "Sodom and its daughters" (Ezekiel 16). The occurrence of Zoar or Bab edh-Dhr'a as a main city and Mazra'a and Mekhoza as satellite settlements is a reasonable model. Shift of a settlement's name together with part of its functions from the main city to a satellite could have happened during the past. The greater dimension of the sea during 19th and 20th centuries A.D. when much of the south basin was flooded as compared with its size during Roman times probably biased the attitude of geographers in identifying Zoar at Es-Safi. These data should be considered impartially but the problem remains unsolved.

Uncertainty in positions of the city of Sodom, the Pillar of Salt (Lot's Wife), the city of Zoar, the settlement of Es-Safi at the delta of Wadi Hasa (Hesa), and the Zered River should be expected. The long histories of habitation, at least 5,000 years, and long cultural gaps related to physical changes of climate, lake level, and tectonic subsidence of the basin must be considered. The longest cultural gaps are for Sodom and Gomorrah whose precise positions remain undiscovered and whose ruins could not be studied archaeologically. The second longest gap is for Bab edh-Dhr'a which remained unoccupied between the end of the Early Bronze age and the Hellenistic time. The possibility is raised by

Braslavy (1956, pp. 322–23) that its position may have been shifted after submergence beneath Dead Sea water and cover by new sediments.

Even if a conquering nation preserved and continued the culture of a conquered one, such as during the later transitions from Second Temple to Roman-Byzantine and from Byzantine to Moslem times, some confusion may occur including mistakes in site identification. Perhaps Eusebius, a 4th-century A.D. geographer of a conquering nation and not as deeply rooted in biblical history, was more likely to make a mistake than the 1st-century A.D. Josephus (1959, *The Jewish Wars*). In spite of valuable contributions by these two authors, both made errors. Hieronymus, a translator of the Bible (the Vulgate), lived from the 4th to the 5th century A.D. and had extensive knowledge and a pedantic approach and was motivated to devote a decade of his lifetime to this work because of the many mistakes he found in earlier translations (Encyclopaedia Hebraica, 1960, 14:30–34).

Sodom City and Mount Sedom

No physical traces mark the precise position of the city of Sodom but it may be inferred that it was near Mount Sedom. The diapiric rise of the salt mountain, its asymmetry toward the east (Zak, 1967), a left-lateral fault movement along its north-south axis (Figure 1.4), and deep subsidence of the sediment-filled basin east of the diapir indicate the probability that a great earthquake was responsible for the thorough destruction of Sodom.

Earliest mention of rocksalt quarrying at Mount Sedom is implied by the literal meaning of the Hebrew word in a verse in which the sterile nature of Sodom and Gomorrah is compared to a "salt mine" (Zephaniah 2:9), although the term used in the English translation of the Bible refers to "saltpit." The "salt mine" interpretation is corroborated in a commentary by Jonathan Ben-Uziel (Braslavy, 1956, p. 98). Claudius Galenus, a famous 2nd-century A.D. Greek physician, used the term "Sodom-salt" in association with the "Sodom mountains which are close to the Dead Sea" (quoted by Braslavy). Mining of salt also can be inferred from two cargo ships shown on the Madaba mosaic of 6th century A.D. (Avi-Yonah, 1953; Figure 5.1) carrying white as well as pink loads (Bloch, 1962) presumably from the south toward Jericho. Commercial rocksalt quarrying from Mount Sedom was practiced occasionally until the early 20th century. Its quality was better than that produced by evaporation of Dead Sea brine, as it was devoid of the bitter taste associated with high magnesium-chloride content of brine.

It could be inferred from the two versions of Talmudic discussions (3rd century A.D.) concerning the distance between the cities of Sodom and Zoar that Rabbi Hannina Bar-Hamma was personally acquainted with the area and knew the positions of these two sites (Jerusalem Tal-

Figure 5.1. Mosaic map of the Dead Sea made at Madaba about A.D. 560 (Avi-Yonah, 1953). Note that Zoar is at the southeast corner of the sea and there is no indication of Lisan Peninsula and south basin, as though water level then was below −400 m m.s.l. The two ships may be carrying salt to Jericho but the artist has put the steering oars at the bow instead of the stern of the ships. Perhaps the cargoes are merchandise to be traded for salt.

mud, Berakhot Tractate p. 4b and Babylonian Talmud, Pesahim Tractate, p. 93b). The term "Sodom and her daughters" is mentioned several times in Ezekiel 16:53, 55, probably not just for literary purposes. Agricultural communities could have existed both south and north of Mount Sedom and salt mines functioned along its east flanks.

Pillar of Salt—Lot's Wife

A slim, several tens of meters tall joint block of vertically tilted rocksalt layers on the east flank of Mount Sedom (Figure 3.3) is locally identified as the site and image of Lot's wife. The top few meters of that pillar consists of a horizontal finely stratified sequence of gypsum and marl that unconformably overlies a salt table (Gary et al., 1974), the whole giving the impression of a statue. Other possible candidates for Lot's Wife are abundant along that flank, a "harem of wives" (Blankenhorn, 1898, as quoted by Braslavy, 1956, p. 96). It is not surprising that this feature or its predecessors has been so identified and described by many geographers and pilgrims since Josephus in the 1st century A.D. (1906, *Antiquities*, pt. 1, 11: 4). The pillars consist mostly of easily soluble rocksalt so their durability is brief and collapse occurs. The weak point of this view is their close proximity to Mount Sedom and presumably to the city of Sodom. Such location disagrees with the text describing the transformation of Lot's wife as if the pillar were near the city of Zoar. The description implies that Lot, his wife and their two daughters had already crossed "all the plain" on their way from Sodom to Zoar (Genesis 19:17, 23, 26).

If the suggestion by Albright et al. (1944) to identify the location of Zoar at the Early Bronze III site of Bab edh-Dhr'a is correct, the biblical pillar of salt should be sought near the east flank of the Lisan Peninsula. Although at present no such feature is known on the peninsula, a past existence there during the Early Bronze age is plausible. Lisan Peninsula was formed by diapiric rise of a rocksalt body from the underlying depocenter of the Dead Sea graben between Miocene–Early Pliocene and Recent times (Nasr, 1949; Neev and Emery, 1967; Neev and Hall, 1979). Some form of rocksalt subcrops the Lisan Formation and is exposed at the northeast corner of the peninsula or along the west coast of the Bay of Mazra'a (Braslavy, 1956, p. 82). Its elevation at that point is similar to that of rocksalt penetrated by a Lisan I deep drill hole at Anomaly A (Figure 1.4; Neev and Emery, 1967, fig. 10; Zak, 1967). Closely spaced photolineaments were identified along the east flanks of an oval-shaped northeast-southwest-trending domal structure (Anomaly B of Nasr, 1949). Morphology of these lineaments is described as a "... succession of parallel shallow synclines and flat anticlinal axes ..." (Nasr, 1949, p. 12).

Similar features at the crest of Mount Sedom were formed by se-

lective solution of vertical rocksalt layers forming parallel linear syncli-
nal grooves alternating with more resistant marl and sandstone layers
(Zak, 1967). It is assumed that lineaments at Mount Sedom are genetically analogous to the photolineaments at Anomaly B on the Lisan
Peninsula—both representing nearly vertical rocksalt strata. In both
areas these beds were repetitively truncated by diluted brines of Lisan
Lake and the Dead Sea during wet climatic phases as indicated by low
flat relief of Anomaly B and by the east-tilted salt table at the top of
Mount Sedom. It is clear that pillars of salt occasionally could have been
formed and destroyed near the southeast corner of the Lisan Peninsula
during historic and prehistoric times.

Local residents in the region named several 10- to 20-m-tall weath-
ered red sandstone pinnacles either Lot's wife, Lot's daughter, or Lot's
dog, depending on the angle of view or light-and-shadow conditions
(Almog and Eshel, 1949, pp. 240–41). These consist of Paleozoic Nubian
sandstone and are about 10 km north-northeast of Mazra'a at different
elevations across the East border fault escarpment of the sea (Figure
1.4). Heavy paraffinic or ozokerite oil is seeping in several places at the
foot of the Nubian sandstone fault escarpment along that segment of
the coast (Picard, 1943, and personal communication).

City of Zoar

The biblical story relates that Zoar is the only one of the five cities of
the plain spared from being overthrown and destroyed during the
disastrous Sodom and Gomorrah event. Lot found his first shelter at Zoar
and the next day continued fleeing east to the Moab and Ammon mountains (Figure 1.3). Both of these mountain areas and the two nations
that dwelt there were named later after Lot's two sons born after the
event (Genesis 19:30–38), implying that Zoar was near the east margin
of the Dead Sea south basin. Beyond that interpretation, opinions are
split as to its exact location. At present Zoar's most widely accepted
position is close to the village of Es-Safi near the southeast corner of
the basin on the south part or lobe of the alluvial fan of Wadi Hasa (Figures 1.3, 1.4, 4.15, 5.1).

There are reasons to favor this south approach. Eusebius, bishop of
Caesarea, in *Onomastikon* (Melamed, 1966) identified Nimrim (Isaiah
15:6 and Jeremiah 48:34) as a small village located north of Zoar. Nimrim
is Numeira (Figures 1.3, 1.4) situated between Bab edh-Dhr'a on the
north and Es-Safi at the south. Dimasqui noted in A.D. 1300 that Zoar is
known also as Es-Safi (Marmardji, 1951, p. 48). According to the Madaba
mosaic map (Avi-Yonah, 1953) and a description by Josephus (1959,
The Jewish Wars), Zoar of Roman-Byzantine days was at the southeast
or south limit of the Dead Sea. It is possible that scholars of the late 19th
and early 20th centuries A.D. were biased to adopt "the south approach"

because the sea level during their lifetime was so high that the shore-line approached the village of Es-Safi. Although identifications of that site by Eusebius and Dimasqui are clear and should not be dismissed lightly, these three site locations should be accepted only after judging an alternative interpretation.

Scripts engraved on four tombstones from a Jewish cemetery near Es-Safi imply that an important Jewish community existed there during the 4th to 6th centuries A.D. (Almog and Eshel, 1949, pp. 17–20, figs. A, B). Since the name of Zoar was not mentioned in any of these scripts, they cannot serve as evidence for its identification at this location.

General topography of the Dead Sea supports a north approach for the Early Bronze site of Zoar at Bab edh-Dhr'a on the basis of study of paleo sea levels. The south coast of the sea always was more subject to large horizontal shifts than other coastal segments because its bottom slopes very gently toward the north. A southward increase of about 35 km in the length of the sea should have occurred during Climatic Wet Phase III following the Intermediate Bronze age when the water level rose about 100 m. The south coastline then shifted from the Lisan Peninsula to the Amazyahu escarpment (Figure 1.4). Identification of Zoar at Es-Safi based on the description by Josephus could be acceptable only for wet climatic phases or subphases when the level was high enough to reach −390 m m.s.l. or higher. Such identification during the lifetime of Josephus requires the climates of 1st century A.D. to be known. Average regional temperatures during Early to Late Roman times (200 B.C. to A.D. 100) probably were higher than at present (Neumann, 1991, 1992). The east-west Roman road (Figures 1.2, 2.1, 4.15) crossing Lynch Strait and the peninsula was first paved during the reign of Traianus (Trajan) Caesar in A.D. 106 as a branch of the north-south Kings Highway along the Jordanian highland (Har-El, 1971, p. 35). The strait was crossable then because the south shore of the sea was north of the peninsula. As Zoar of the 1st century A.D. was a seaport, it had to be on the shore and must have been north of that transverse road or near the head of the Bay of Mazra'a. The absence of any graphic indication for the pensinula's existence on the Madaba map (Figure 5.1; Avi-Yonah, 1953) leads to a similar conclusion. Such an outstanding and picturesque tonguelike shore would not have been overlooked by the artist-cartographer of that map.

Importantly, Zoar was a harbor. Commercial maritime transportation is known to have functioned in the Dead Sea at least since Hellenistic times (Nissenbaum, 1990) and has never completely ceased since then. Postures of two cargo vessels portrayed on the Madaba map imply that the main traffic was between Zoar, port at the southeast corner of the north basin and the north coast as close as possible to Jericho, the gate to Judea. The Bay of Mazra'a was always the main if not the only natural deepwater haven, although exposed to northerly storms. It still is named *al minna*, the port in Arabic, and was protected during Byzantine time by a small fortress locally named *al Karia*, the city in Arabic, Aramaic, and Hebrew, situated on a steep hill at the north tip of the peninsula (Braslavy, 1956, pp. 288–90). If Zoar were at Es-Safi (Figures 1.2, 1.3, 1.4), it never could have functioned as an efficient harbor. This conclusion is evident from a vivid description of the landing adventure experienced by engineers of Palestine Potash Ltd. in 1932 at Es-Safi when the sea level was at −392 m m.s.l., very nearly the −391.5 m 1896 peak of that stage. The several-meter-long motorboat named *Yettomah* brought them about 2 km from the shore and some of the passengers continued toward land aboard a smaller flat-bottom paddle-wheeler. Then an even smaller rowboat and small raft were used to land (Almog and Eshel, 1949, p. 179). A few years later when potassium products had to be shipped north from the plant at the southwest flank of the basin, the lake bottom was deepened by dredging and a few-hundred-meter-long pier was built at Mount Sedom so that cargo could be loaded there.

Existence of Zoar at the Bay of Mazra'a in the days of Babta (A.D. 132) is inferred from the contents of a bundle of more than 40 papyrus legal documents recently found in a karstic cave within the main fault escarpment high above the Dead Sea where residents of En Gedi found refuge during the Bar-Kokhba revolt against Rome. Most of these belonged to an elderly lady named Babta and dealt with real-estate issues. They were written between late 1st century A.D. and A.D. 132. This woman was identified in a document of A.D. 130 as "Babta, the daughter of Simon from Mekhoza of Zoar in the province of Petra who dwells at her home in the same Mekhoza" (Yadin, 1971, pp. 233, 244, 248). She fled from there to En Gedi at the beginning of the revolt. This quotation implies that Mekhoza and Zoar were very near and related to each other. *Mekhoza* in Aramaic, Hebrew, and Arabic means a haven, port, or harbor (Even-Shoshan, 1969, p. 1289; Kutscher, 1974, pp. 41–45; Broshi, 1990), suggesting that Mekhoza of that time was the prime active port of the Dead Sea. The settlement of Mazra'a also is mentioned in a document dated 9 June A.D. 130 (Yadin, 1971, p. 248), the same name today for an Arab village situated at the head of the Bay of Mazra'a (Figures 1.4, 4.15). It is assumed that during the lifetime of Babta the towns Zoar, Mekhoza, and Mazra'a were clustered around the bay even though they existed as three separate entities.

The "north approach" locating Zoar near the Bay of Mazra'a or close to Bab edh-Dhr'a seems to be at least as convincing as reasons favoring the south alternative for it at Es-Safi. Broshi (1990, p. 272) rejected this suggestion by Neev and Emery (1967) because this town is now the most important population center of the region. At present the qualitative and quantitative agricultural prerequisites for a settlement there are superior to the area of Mazra'a. Its alluvial fan has a perennial and most prolific water supply from Wadi Hasa with very low content of dissolved solids; consequently the area is lush and suitable for agriculture. Ruins of several water-driven sugar mills apparently from Moslem, Crusader, and Mamluk cultures are at the mouth of Wadi Hasa (Almog and Eshel, 1949). This difference between the two oases may not have been so prominent during Roman and earlier times as it is today. Braslavy (1956, pp. 378–79) described ruins of several of these mills in the Bay of Mazra'a. They were fed by water flowing from the mouth of Wadi Karak (Wadi Sail edh-Dhr'a). Braslavy quoted two European geographers (without reference) who identified an 80-m-long and 8-m-broad relict of an aqueduct along the east coast of that bay leading to Roman-Byzantine ruins in the Plain (Ghor) of Haditha north of Mazra'a. A well-built 6- to 7-m-wide Roman road paralleling the aqueduct leads northeast to the Jordanian Plateau. These installations functioned during Roman, Byzantine, and Early Moslem times, indicating that the Bay of Mazra'a then was densely populated and economically active with a much more prolific water supply than at present. Its soils must have been productive at times especially after extensive rainy seasons when they were flushed thoroughly.

Distance between Sodom and Zoar has been a source of argument since Roman times. Jewish scholars of the 3rd century A.D. were faced with interpretational difficulties in correlating the timetable of the Sodom saga with distance between these two cities. Relevant verses of the story (Genesis 19:15–16, 23) are as follows: "As dawn broke, the angel urged Lot on, saying: 'Up, take your wife and two remaining daughters, lest you be swept away because of the iniquity of the city.' Still he delayed. So the angels seized his hand, and the hands of his wife and his two daughters—in the LORD's mercy on him—and brought him out and left him outside the city. . . . As the sun rose upon the earth, Lot entered Zoar." Klein (1986, pp. 29, 34) quoted only the Babylonian version of the Talmud (Pesahim Tractate, p. 93b) regarding the distance between Sodom and Zoar. That version implies that Rabbi Hannina Bar-Hamma had seen this area personally and considered the distance to be 5 miles or 7.4 km—the length of a straight line between the south end of Mount Sedom and the village of Es-Safi (Figures 1.3, 1.4, 4.15). The same question recurs in a different version in the Jerusalem Talmud (Berakhot Tractate, 1st chapter, p. 4b), from which it sounds as if Jerusalem scholars still were bothered by that problem in spite of Rabbi Hannina's statement. Their rationale to solve the dilemma reads as follows: "Said Rabbi Hazna: Between dawn (the rise of the morning star) and the first light in the east until the rise of the sun upon the earth—4 miles. . . . And from Sodom to Zoar 4 miles? Does this mean that the distance between Sodom and Zoar is only 4 miles? We know that there are more there." Said Rabbi Ze'ira: "The angel was bridging (the way) before them." This explanation in biblical texts infers that walking speeds of humans and angels were not the same.

A similar difference is recorded in another story in which an even longer time difference is involved. This supposedly happened less than one day before the destructive event at Sodom and Gomorrah (Genesis 18:1–15, 22, 33; 19:1) as follows: Close to noon time ("in the heat of the day") three angels in the image of people suddenly approached the tent of Abraham when he dwelt at Alonei (the oak trees of) Mamr'e near the city of Hebron. The hospitable patriarch did his best to treat them well, letting them wash and rest, preparing new bread for them, catching a tender calf, dressing it, preparing a good meal, and serving them properly. After dinner the guests conversed with Abraham at length and blessed his wife Sarah, saying that within a year she would have a son. By late (?) afternoon the angels continued their way to Sodom, and Abraham went with them to bring them on the way. "And there came two angels to Sodom at even [evening]; and Lot sat in the gate of Sodom: and Lot seeing them rose up to meet them." A direct line between Hebron and the northmost plunge of Mount Sedom is more than 50 km and the distance between Hebron and the nearest part of the Dead Sea is about 30 km. Unless heavenly powers are involved it is impossible for normal people to cross such an area on foot to reach Sodom from Hebron during the very few hours of daylight that were left.

The record that Lot, his wife, and his two daughters walked from Sodom to Zoar means that at that time the level of the Dead Sea had to be so low as to expose the floor of Lynch Strait and that the destruction of Sodom and Gomorrah followed a long period of hot, dry climate.

Zoar—Key to Moab

Zoar is referred to by Isaiah within "the burden of Moab" (Isaiah 15:5–6): "My heart shall cry out for Moab; her fugitives shall flee unto Zoar, a heifer of three years old: for the mounting up of Luhith with weeping shall they go it up; for in the way of Horonaim they shall raise up a cry of destruction. For the water of Nimrim shall be desolate." A similar chapter (Jeremiah 48:6) reads: "For in the going up of Luhith continual weeping shall go up; for in the going down of Horonaim the enemies have heard a cry of destruction." The Hebrew word *brikheiha* (her latches or bars) was translated in the English version of the Bible as "fugitives" (Isaiah 15:5). The cause of this confusion could be the phonetical similarity of the terms *brikhim* (latches) and *borkhim* (fugitives).

This explanation was first expressed in the Vulgate, the Latin translation of the Bible made by Hieronymus (Munster, 1542). He commented on that subject, as quoted by Braslavy (1956, pp. 382–83, although without a reference) by comparing the strategic importance of

Zoar, the gate to Moab, to that of Jericho, the bar or gate to the land of Israel. Hieronymus supported his own version (*brikhim* = latches) by quoting Midrash Rabba (A.D. 426 to 500) in which Rabbi Samuel Bar Nahmani compared Jericho to the gate of Israel. The terms bar or gate are authorized meanings of the Aramaic-Hebrew term *negarra* used in that Midrash (Even-Shoshan, 1969). On the other hand Munster (1542) in his own Latin translation interpreted the term *brikheiha* as fugitives. That same problem is avoided by the Greek translation, the Septuagint of 3rd century B.C., indicating the involved uncertainty. The relevant sentence in that translation (Isaiah 15:5) reads as follows: "The heart of Moab cries from the inside unto Segor (Zoar)" (translated by Dr. Vasilius Tzaferis, Israel Authority of Antiquities, Jerusalem, personal communication).

Description of the west approaches to Moab as "the latches of Moab" is striking in its reality as it perfectly fits the physiography of that region. The Hebrew text uses the words *Ma'aleh HaLuhith* in both Isaiah 15:5 and Jeremiah 48:5 whose precise meaning is the mountainous pass of Luhith. Unfortunately this term was omitted in some translations. The entire border fault escarpment of the rift along the east side of the Dead Sea is especially steep and hard to cross except east of Lisan Peninsula, where the strata are tilted down toward the south, west, and north from their nearly horizontal position beneath the Jordanian plateau. This funnel-shaped flexure creates more gradual topographic gradients than elsewhere along the east escarpment and is focused near Bab edh-Dhr'a to form a unique natural pass from the Dead Sea to the Moab mountains (Figures 1.2, 1.3, 1.4, 2.1, 4.15; Neev and Emery, 1967, p. 34, figs. 8, 13, 18).

Three ancient roads climb from the east side of the Lisan Peninsula toward the Jordanian Plateau (Figures 2.1, 4.15). The central road, Luhith Pass, leads east from Bab edh-Dhr'a toward Karak. Its lowest segment winds across a west steeply dipping "flatiron," one of several formed along a crescentic fault-fold line. From the line of flatirons the road climbs gradually along the Karak monocline, a moderate and uniform west dipslope of Middle Cretaceous strata up to Karak—a rise of 900 m along a distance of 14 km or a slope of about 7°. It fits perfectly the biblical Hebrew term for this road, "the Ascent (or Pass) of Luhith," because the meaning of the last word in Hebrew is a table or board, agreeing with images of both a flatiron and the uninterrupted dipslope down the Cretaceous dolomitic strata. According to the *Onomastikon* of Eusebius, the 4th-century A.D. bishop of Caesarea, Luhith "is a village between Ar-Moab (or Kir-Moab—Karak) and Zoar" (Melamed, 1966). The recent name of Bab edh-Dhr'a is meaningful as it is a gate in Arabic, a term often used for the narrow entrance of a road from open and flat territory into a mountainous one such as Bab el Wad where the road enters a narrow wadi on its way up from the west coastal plain toward Jerusalem. Such a setup agrees with Isaiah's expression "her latches reach unto Zoar."

The second road is the Ascent of Horonaim (Isaiah 14:5–6), which climbs southeast from the southmost corner of Lisan Peninsula neck to join Kings Highway at Mauta about 1 km above m.s.l. and 10 km south of Karak (Figures 1.2, 1.3, 1.4, 4.15). Kings Highway (Aharoni, 1964b, maps 10, 13) is along the north-south-trending crest of the Jordanian highland plateau or west of it. One segment of the Ascent of Horonaim is beautifully shown on an oblique airphoto taken by Glueck (1937, p. 148, and fig. 24 in Har-El, 1962, 1971). It is marked on the Biblical Road Map of Israel as the road that leaves Kings Highway about 10 km south of Karak, descends toward the Lisan Peninsula, crosses Lynch Strait, and climbs west to Judea. Horonaim also is mentioned in the script of Mesha king of Moab and Jeremiah 48:5 as the Descent of Horonaim.

The third road is a trail that climbs from the alluvial fan of Ghor El-Haditha along the east coast of the Bay of Mazra'a northeast to join Kings Highway about 15 km north of Karak. Remains of the wide Roman road along the bay are part of that road at present.

Zered River

The Zered River was almost unanimously identified by Bible scholars and geographers of the 19th and 20th centuries A.D. as Wadi Hasa east of Es-Safi (Figures 1.2, 1.3, 4.15). The rationale of this correlation is similar to that for locating Zoar at this location. Use was made of the Madaba map (Figure 5.1; Avi Yonah, 1953) on which Zered River is marked as west-descending about one-fifth of the Dead Sea length north of the southeast end of the sea. In modern maps the alleged outlet of the Zered River (or Wadi Hasa) from the mountains into the plain is at the south end of the sea or slightly south of the ancient tel of Es-Safi (Figure 1.4). Wadi Hasa is one of the most prominent east-west-trending natural boundaries dividing the Jordanian highlands and is designated as the most acceptable boundary between Edom (Mount Se'ir) and Moab (Aharoni, 1964b, maps 8, 10, 52, 68, 69, 118, 120).

The Zered River is described by Eusebius (Melamed, 1966) to be "at the edge of the wilderness." The "wilderness of Edom and Moab" gradually develops toward the east of the crest of the Jordanian high-lands. Most of it is a north-south-trending belt beyond Wilderness High-way (Figure 1.2) and the present railway to Aqaba and Saudi Arabia. The east-west-trending Wadi Hasa is not at the edge of the Wilderness but perpendicular to it, in much better agreement with biblical descriptions as well as relevant paragraphs in the *Onomasticon* of Eusebius. Accordingly Zered is a tributary that flows north from a point east of Karak to join the east-west-trending Arnon River about midway be-tween the Dead Sea and Wilderness Highway (Figures 1.2, 1.3, 4.15). Both rivers and related subjects are described at least twice in the Bible. Numbers 21:10–13 reads "The Israelites marched on and camped at Oboth. They set out from Oboth and camped at Iye-abaraim, in the wilderness bordering on Moab to the east. From there they set out and encamped at the Valley of Zered. From there they set out and encamped beyond the Arnon, that is, in the wilderness that extends from the territory of the Amorites." Deuteronomy 2:8–9, 13, 19 states, "[W]e marched on in the direction of the wilderness of Moab. And the LORD said to me: 'Do not harass the Moabites or engage them in war. For I will not give you any of their land as a possession; I have given Ar as a possession to the descendents of Lot. . . . Up now! Cross the Brook Zered.' So we crossed the Wadi Zered. . . . 'You will then be close to the Ammonites; do not harass them or start a fight with them. For I will not give any part of the land of the Ammonites to you as a possession; I have given it as a possession to the descendents of Lot.'"

The description, if carefully read, clearly outlines the northerly route of the wandering children of Israel along the east territory of Moab at the boundary between sown land and desert. They reached as far as the perennial Zered River, then crossed north through Arnon River near the boundary between the Moabites and Amorites continuing northeast to bypass the Ammonites. Ammon is situated beyond the northeast corner of Moab and east of the Amorites (Gordon, 1975, p. 17). This implies that the northmost reach of the Zered River joins the west-flowing Arnon River at the triple junction of the Moabite, Amorite, and Ammonite kingdoms. Zered should not be confused with west-flowing Wadi Hasa about 20 km south of Karak.

Erroneous identification of the Zered River was first recognized by I. Horowitz (1923, p. 27) who based his interpretation on Jonathan Ben-Uziel's translation of the Bible into Aramaic about 24 B.C. Horowitz's commentary reads as follows: "Zered. A river. One of the camps of the children of Israel. Named in later days Nahal (River) Tarvaia." Horowitz connected this term with the present name of perennial Wadi al Tar-fawiye on a map by Fischer, Guthe, and Dalman (undated), a slightly distorted version of the Aramaic name *Tarvaia* for a north-flowing tributary of the Arnon River (Wadi Mojib) starting about 20 km east of Karak. The Hebrew word *zered* means sprout, twig, or a kind of bush eaten by animals. *Tarfawiya* seems to have the same root as *taraf* in Hebrew meaning fresh or new vegetation. *Tarfa* in Arabic means tamarisk and *tarfa* in Aramaic is leaf or bud. Braslavy (1956, p. 331) considered that the Arabic and Aramaic word *tarfa* associated with the Hebrew term *zered* resembles the Greek word *tarphea*, meaning weeds or thicket of bushes. Phonetically this Greek name is even closer to *tarfawiya* and argues in favor of Horowitz's interpretation. These linguistic data favor the correlation between Wadi Tarfawiya and the Zered River. It appears that the term Zared on the Madaba map was extended to encompass both the Arnon River and its tributary, the Zered River.

6

Sodom and Gomorrah Event

About 7800 B.P. after the first effects of warmings and droughts associated with the Atlantic Interval, many people of the Mideast moved into river floodplains where suitable agricultural soils and freshwater were available. Prominent examples are in Mesopotamia, the Nile Valley, and along the Jordan–Dead Sea rift. The extremely dry climates occasionally improved because of small fluctuations within the Chalcolithic and a larger one during Early Bronze II, when there was a 250-year wet interval (Figures 3.2, 3.6). These climatic changes explain the settling, flourishing, and abandonment by the Ghassulians about 6000 B.C. and of the city of Arad, 4900 to 4650 B.P. at the fringe of the desert (R. Amiran and Gophna, 1989, n. 18; D. Amiran, 1991; Gilead, 1993).

During the Early Bronze ages overall the climatic conditions in the Dead Sea region were not appreciably different from those at present, as attested by fossil flora found in excavations at Bab edh-Dhr'a and Numeira (McCreery, 1980). High yields of agriculture in fertile irrigated areas were an incentive to settle in the Plain of Sodom. This settling gradually intensified within the fertile plains of the Jordan–Dead Sea region as well as in Canaan through Early Bronze I and II but weakened toward the end of Early Bronze III. This is indicated by the pattern of settlements that developed from individual villages to city-states with satellite villages—mostly because of economic and social motivations—which later were changed into fortified communities (Esse, 1989).

A gradual increase in fortification of Early Bronze settlements along the Dead Sea and Jordan Valley basins and the position of some of them along the narrow elevated step-faulted strip of the east foothills (Zori, 1962; Ben-Arieh, 1965; Rast, 1987 and personal communication, 1989) indicate increased need for defense by settlers against raids and invasions. These evidences of stress probably resulted from gradual climatic drying and warming. Investments in defense facilities were worthwhile if increased productivity was tempting enough. Such areas could have been found not only along the east foothills but also at the foot of the Amazyahu fault escarpment and in the delta of Nahal Zohar north of Mount Sedom (Figure 4.15) if fresh or slightly brackish water was available there during the Early Bronze age. Mining of tradable rocksalt from Mount Sedom could have been a favorable economic venture at least since the Chalcolithic age (Bloch, 1962), encouraging people to settle also along the west flank of the basin.

A relatively quiet tectonic regime during Early and Middle Holocene Period or Late Neolithic to Early Bronze III, a 3,500-year span, contributed to prosperous environments for human occupation within the plains of Sodom, Beth She'an, and Kinneret. It ended near the close of Early Bronze III when Sodom and Gomorrah were destroyed by earthquakes.

Complete disruption of both mud-brick houses and municipal installations of settlements could have resulted from release of intense seismic energy, as insinuated by specific expressions that describe the destruction of Sodom and Gomorrah: "He overthrew those cities and all the Plain, and all the inhabitants of the cities, and that which grew upon the ground." Such unique and strong expression with respect to an earthquake is used in the Bible only regarding the traumatic event of Sodom and Gomorrah. The destructive potential of earthquake energy affecting the trough of a basin filled with uncompacted sediments would be much greater than along its solid perimeter, as illustrated by the 20th-century earthquakes at Mexico City, San Francisco, and Los Angeles. The Sodom and Gomorrah event could have been even more severe because other factors were involved in it, such as the gliding of sedimentary fill toward the center of the basin along the downthrown side of the Amazyahu growth fault. Biblical script derived from oral tradition of the disruption of Sodom and Gomorrah as a supernatural event should not be dismissed as an exaggerated fictitous story written to satisfy religious motives.

An outburst of smoke and rain of sulfurous fire reportedly accompanied the destruction of Sodom and Gomorrah (Genesis 19:24, 28). These materials are interpreted as products of light fractions of hydrocarbons escaping from underground reservoirs and igniting upon reaching the surface. Presence of heavier hydrocarbons in the Dead Sea subsurface is proved by numerous recent seepages as well as by the tar pits described in Genesis 14:10. Source rocks for these gases, oil, and asphalt are in bituminous marls and limestones of Late Cretacaeous Period buried within the graben as well as the organic matter in overlying sediments of the Dead Sea Group (Figure 6.1 Top; Clapp, 1936; Nissenbaum and Goldberg, 1980; Rullkötter, Spiro, and Nissenbaum, 1985; Tannenbaum and Aizenshtat, 1985; Aizenshtat, Mileslavski, and Tannenbaum, 1986). The 'hydrocarbon fraction' could have been cracked and released from its source rocks because of deep burial and geothermal heating beneath the 6- to 10-km thickness of sediments of the Tertiary to Recent Dead Sea Group. Asphalts probably were released near the margins of the graben and oils close to the axis where the sediments were thicker and the temperature higher. Rejuvenated faulting associated with the Sodom and Gomorrah earthquake would have opened numerous channels for sudden escape of hydrocarbons, allowing much larger outbursts and fires.

Late Cretaceous marls contain up to 35% of organic matter in which sulfur may reach 10%. Contact of acidic hot brines with buried carbonate rocks could produce carbon dioxide. Percolation of hot brines through highly fractured source rocks and immature asphalt would have reduced much of their sulfur content. Combination of these components may produce a highly pressurized mixture of gasified liquid hydrocarbon rich in sulfur and hydrogen sulfide. This mixture when burned probably would emit large volumes of thick black smoke capable of being seen from great distances as from Hebron, about 60 km from Sodom Plain. Sulfur dioxide could generate a fallout of concentrated acidic rain resulting in mass mortality of animals—including people—and vegetation in areas near the bitumen seeps.

Bentor (1989) had a different interpretation. He correctly stated that modern use of the Hebrew word *kittor* in the text means steam and not smoke and fire and the biblical text should be interpreted accordingly. According to Even-Shohan (1969, p. 2336) this word has a dual meaning and the specific expression *kittor* in Genesis 19:28 is "smoke of fire— a pillar of smoke." Bentor explained that steam was produced by the sudden rush of Dead Sea brines onto the exposed hot dry sediments of the south basin because of tectonic subsidence of the sill at Lynch Strait. Although such transgression is not mentioned in the biblical text, it probably happened but only about 350 years after the Sodom and Gomorrah tectonic event of Early Bronze III time—at the end of the Intermediate Bronze age when a significant increase of rainfall caused the sea level to rise.

Most tar seepages are closely associated with border faults of the graben. One recently was found in the south basin near its contact with the rocksalt diapiric structure of the Lisan Peninsula (M. Goldberg, Israel Geological Survey, personal communication). Other such seepages are along the north fringes of the peninsula or elsewhere in the north basin

Figure 6.1. Top. Black concretional layer within Late Cretaceous bituminous marl at Nebi Musa west of the Dead Sea. The marl probably extends east beneath the sea under several kilometers of Tertiary and Quaternary sediments as shown in Figure 2.1. Bottom. A large block of asphalt from the floor of the Dead Sea. It floated to the water surface and drifted to the west shore of the north basin. Photographed by Y. Nir in 1955.

(Figure 6.1 Bottom; Nissenbaum and Goldberg, 1980, pl. 2C), as illustrated by occasional floating in the Dead Sea of large blocks of asphalt to a few tens of tons in weight, presumably released from the bottom of either basin by earth tremors (Nissenbaum, Aizenshtat, and Goldberg, 1979).

Flavius Josephus (1906, 1959) used the term "Lake Asphaltites" several times in his descriptions of the Dead Sea (*Antiquities* VII, X; *Jewish Wars* III, 10,7). This name probably was used by Poseidonius of Aphamia Syria, in the 2nd century B.C. and later by Diodorus of Sicily in the 1st century B.C. (Breslavy, 1956, p. 267). Lynch (1849) observed many fragments of drifted asphalts (bitumens) along the shores of the sea. A modern example of a tar pit occurs at Ein el Hummar in seepages of ozokerite or brown paraffinic wax and heavy oil impregnating outcrops of Paleozoic Nubian sandstone at the foot of the East border fault escarpment between the Arnon River and Lisan Peninsula (Figures 1.4, 2.17). About 30 barrels of light 30 API oil with gas and brines recently flowed from a shallow (300-m) test hole drilled here.

Perhaps "slime (tar) pits"—as described in Genesis 14:10 about the fall of the kings of Sodom and Gomorrah into the pits, trapping them during their flight from the four raiding kings—were more abundant in both basins during Early Bronze III than today. In ancient times this "slime" (*hemar* in Hebrew also means asphalt or bitumen) was used as mortar in buildings, including the Tower of Babel (Genesis 11:3), for paving roads, caulking boats (perhaps including Noah's Ark—Genesis 6:14), medication, and as an adhesive according to Connan, Nissenbaum, and Dessort (1992). Another important use was as a preservative in Egyptian mummies; in fact, the term "mummy" may have come from the Persian word *mummia,* signifying bitumen because of the black appearance of embalmed bodies. Organic geochemical analyses of resistant chemical fossils (biomarkers) have been used in several studies correlating asphalts and resins found in embalming material of many mummies, fragments of their wrapping and their coffins (Rullkötter and Nissembaum, 1988; Connan and Dessort, 1991) with those used for other purposes (Connan et al., 1992) and with those in floating blocks and natural seeps of the Dead Sea. A recent study (L. E. Eglinton, in preparation, Woods Hole Oceanographic Institution) confirmed this by positively correlating asphalt from a floating block with bitumen in Cretaceous shale at Nebi Musa.

Convincing arguments presented by Rast and Schaub (1981) and Donahue (1985, p. 139) support Rast's (1987, p. 194) correlations of time and locus of the Sodom tradition with the Early Bronze age and the Dead Sea south basin. Their findings indicate that both Bab edh-Dhr'a and Numeira experienced two severe destructive earthquakes within a period not longer than 50 years at the end of Early Bronze III about 4350 B.P. Evidence of seismic destruction included large-scale collapse of massive towers and other buildings under which skeletons of at least three persons recently were excavated. Extensive fires were associated with these earthquakes. As a result Numeira was abandoned at the end of Early Bronze III but Bab edh-Dhr'a was resettled immediately by Early Bronze IV people. Most of this city remained in a state of ruin. The newly built site had the form of an open settlement with a different pattern. The new density of occupation was appreciably lower than that of Early Bronze III and the economic base shifted from agriculture to a pastoral way of life. Additional instances of total desertion of Early Bronze III sites and immediate resettling by Intermediate Bronze age people also occurred at Beth Yerah near the southwest corner of the Sea of Galilee, at Jericho, and at the Uvda Valley in southeast Negev.

Donahue (1985, p. 136) suggested that the rejuvenated Early Bronze III tectonic phase continued into the Intermediate Bronze. His tectonic-origin concept is corroborated by Macumber and Head (1991, p. 168) who surmised that 30 m of differential vertical movement occurred during the post-Lisan age across the East border fault at Wadi al-Hammeh about 20 km south of Yarmuk River (Figure 4.1). Their consideration is based on the highest reach of Lisan Lake's level to −180 m m.s.l. measured by Neev and Emery (1967) across the fault escarpment at the southwest Dead Sea region and the highest elevation of −150 m m.s.l. of Lisan Lake terraces at Wadi al-Hammeh. Radiocarbon age of the terraces ranges between 19,000 and 15,000 B.P. Results of two new studies made at the south part of the lake, still within the trough of the graben and not on upthrown blocks of the East or West border faults, also indicate that its highest level was −150 m m.s.l. (Yechieli, 1987; Bowman, 1992). True dimension of the rejuvenated post-Lisan differential vertical movement is still an open question.

A severe drought occurred in Canaan and north Mesopotamia during the latter half of the Intermediate Bronze age (Esse, 1989, p. 93; Kochavi, 1989; Rosen, 1989; Avner, 1990; Gophna, 1992; Weiss et al., 1993). These interpretations of climate change are based mostly on archaeological and cultural considerations, such as the change of economic basis from an urban-agricultural society to a more nomadic-grazing one leading to total desertification of large regions when droughts became extreme. These climate changes are corroborated by gamma-ray logs (Figure 3.2).

The most intensive and longest wet phase during the Holocene Period followed the Intermediate Bronze age according to data recovered from reliable sources. Absolute dates for beginning and ending of this stage are ambiguous for reasons that may be related to radiocarbon dating. Cultural changes noted between Early Bronze III and the Intermediate Bronze ages at the Uvda Valley site do not seem to have been associated with conquest and destruction, so they may have been evolutionary. Change to Climatic Wet Phase III after Intermediate Bronze is described by Avner (1990, p. 133): "subsequent to a brief climatic crisis at the end of the 3rd millennium, the climate improved, allowing the new culture to blossom in the desert and in the more temperate settled region." A similar pattern before and after the invasion and settling of Middle Bronze IIA and IIB Sea People and north Asian communities along the Mediterranean coastal plain of Israel also could have been induced by this wet phase. This pattern could be inferred from the following extracts of Kochavi's (1989) descripton of Middle Bronze urbanization process: "The new towns of Middle Bronze IIA seem to have been established suddenly during one swift urbanization wave . . . implanted upon a desolate country with a disintegrated society of non-urban, mainly nomadic affinities. Re-urbanization was brought to Canaan by seafarers and city dwellers from farther north on the Levantine coast . . . [who] were attracted by the civilization vacuum in Canaan with its as yet unexploited coast."

Similar conclusions were made by Neev et al. (1987) from their study of Holocene tectonism along the Mediterranean coast of Israel. Their data indicate that an uninterrupted depositional regime existed across the present coastline between about 20,000 and 4000 B.P. when brackish-water to swamp sediments accumulated. During the Early Bronze III to Middle Bronze II transition, a differential vertical tectonic movement occurred there for the first time in Holocene, initiating the present coastal fault escarpment. Solidly built Middle Bronze IIA and IIB settlements had been established upon the upthrown east side of the fault line, mostly on virgin sediments. Farther inland, Middle Bronze II settlements commonly were built on top of older ruins after a several-centuries-long hiatus. The rejuvenated pre–Middle Bronze IIA uplift across the coastal zone affected the entire continental block east of it.

Rosen (1989, p. 252) considered that gullies in central Israel deepened during Early Bronze IV or Intermediate Bronze ages because of a climatically induced drop of the regional water table—the onset of a dry regime. The same increased rate of wadi incision and lowering of the regional water table could have been brought about by post–Early Bronze III regional tectonic uplift of the entire continental block east of the Mediterranean coast. It may have been enhanced by later increased rainfall during Climatic Wet Phase III in the Middle Bronze age to the end of the Late Bronze age.

The physical and demographic cultural break between Early Bronze III and Intermediate Bronze ages must be viewed in relation to broader conditions of the latter part of Early Bronze III in the whole of ancient Canaan. Evidence of a pattern of widespread destruction and abandonment is present at many Early Bronze III sites. From an archaeological point of view, this age witnessed one of the most sweeping disruptions in its history (Wright, 1961, p. 86; Kenyon, 1979, p. 134; Rast, 1987, pp. 194–95). This crisis at the close of the Early Bronze age was not limited to this country and adjacent regions but occurred as far away as the coasts of Syria and Lebanon (Gophna, 1992). Transitions from First to Second Kingdoms in Egypt and from Sumerian to Akkadian rules in Mesopotamia are parallel examples. Perhaps a common causative factor such as physical disturbances induced social restlessness. Other authors consider that a cultural-demographic-economic process in Canaan could have been the only cause for the almost total cessation of maritime trade with Egypt during the end of the Old Kingdom (Esse, 1989).

A sequence of natural catastrophies such as severe earthquakes, volcanism, and extreme droughts in the Dead Sea–Jordan Valley and adjacent territories (Bashan basalt) could have been part of a much larger regional sequence of events that brought about the end of Early Bronze civilization. Severe earthquakes that destroyed both Bab edh-Dhr'a and Numeira about 4350 B.P. could have served as a most impressive and memorable local overture to the eventful transition period into Middle Bronze. There is question of why other powerful events, such as the extreme drought for 300 years during the Late Intermediate Bronze age, 4200 to 3900 B.P., as well as the 700-year Climatic Wet Phase III associated with regional volcanic eruptions that followed were not woven into the saga of Sodom and Gomorrah. This has no direct answer. Possibly these later events were at their time less impressive and picturesque than sudden earthquakes in the minds of local communities because they occurred gradually and continued longer. For several decades or centuries, their fatal effects—such as the massive desertion of vast dry farming territories of north Mesopotamia and collapse of the Akkadian Empire that followed, 4200 to 3900 B.P. (Weiss et al., 1993) could have been more detrimental. Similarly, the extreme drought of the late Intermediate Bronze age and the submergence of agricultural lands by the rising level of Dead Sea brine during Climatic Wet Phase III produced more extensive desertion of the south basin than the Sodom and Gomorrah earthquake. Perhaps historical memories of catastrophic results of droughts during Intermediate Bronze time are reflected in biblical stories about back-and-forth wandering of the patriarchs between Canaan and Egypt as well as the 400- or even 700-year stay of the Israelites in Egypt.

General duration of Climatic Wet Phase III in the post–Intermediate Bronze age and its intensity of change are deduced mostly from thickness of the marl layer in the Dead Sea south basin for that time and from the presence of four oak samples from Mount Sedom caves. The date when this wet phase ended is more ambiguous than its beginning; the possibility that it could have lasted until the end of Late Bronze should not be dismissed. The assumed genetic relationship between occurrences of wet climatic conditions and phases of volcanic eruptions with tectonic activity on a regional or global scale is speculative yet these events could have been related.

7

Synopsis

Climatic Fluctuations, Tectonic Disturbances, and Cultural Breaks since Late Pleistocene

The two large lakes named Samra and Lisan existed in the Dead Sea graben from 350,000 to 120,000 B.P. and 60,000 to 12,000 B.P. Their sediments tentatively are correlated with the European Riss and Würm glacial epochs. Thick marls are the chief sediments in the deep water north basin. Rocksalt deposition dominated within the troughs of both north and south basins throughout the intervening Riss-Würm Interglacial stage. Lithology of Lisan Formation (Würm) in that basin indicates rapid and extreme fluctuations of level. Eight major climatic cycles are recorded (Figures 3.1, 4.16) during Würm glaciation when the level fluctuated between –180 m m.s.l. and probably lower than –400 m m.s.l. Rocksalt was deposited within both basins during warm dry phases of the Lisan stage. At the present state of knowledge no specific tectonic or volcanic activities can be tied to these climatic events.

The Holocene Period was similar lithologically to that of the Lisan Formation and transition between them was gradual. Primarily the difference between the two was change in relative time span between alternate wet and dry phases. Dry phases of Holocene gradually became longer while wet ones with Dead Sea transgressions became shorter. Tectonic regimes during the first part—the Natufian age to Early Bronze III, 12,000 to 4400 B.P.—seem to have been milder than later ones, end of Early Bronze III to the present. The severe earthquake that destroyed Sodom and Gomorrah in 4350 B.P. was followed by a 300-year long subphase of gradually warming climate that became extremely dry during the latter part of the Intermediate Bronze age. Climatic Wet Phase III began about 3900 B.P. It was the longest, about 800 years, and most intense wet phase of Holocene and it probably was associated with volcanism.

Correlation of Climates and Cultural Demography during Holocene

No abrupt cultural or demographic changes are known during transition from Epi-Paleolithic or Geometric Kebaran from the last glacial phase of the Pleistocene Period through Natufian to the early part of Holocene Pre-Pottery Neolithic. The reason for this stability is not clear especially because average temperatures of global oceans during the latest Pleistocene glaciation were appreciably lower than those during Early Holocene (Emiliani, 1978). Three cycles of climatic fluctuation were recorded in Denmark between 13,000 and 10,000 B.P. (Gary, McAfee, and Wolf, 1974; Berger and Labeyrie, 1987). Since about 8,000 years ago the severity of cultural and demographic breaks increased probably because of greater abruptness of transitions from cold wet conditions to warm dry ones. Although the frequency of these events appears to have increased during the Holocene, there is little doubt that Climatic Wet Phase III, Middle Bronze II to the end of the Late Bronze ages, was the most intense and longest. Beginnings of that wet phase and associated volcanic activities occurred only 450 years after the severe earthquakes of Sodom and Gomorrah at the end of Early Bronze III and after the 350-year long Intermediate Bronze age that had even drier climatic conditions than the rest of the Early Bronze age.

Tectonic or seismic destructions of population centers during Intermediate Bronze age probably occurred at the same time along the Dead Sea rift and Mesopotamia and along the Mediterranean coasts of Syria, Lebanon, and Canaan. This tectonism may have initiated the first phase of emergence of the upthrown side along the Israeli coast during the Holocene.

Three types of massive migrations of people were associated with changes in climatic conditions. The first occurred in moderate circumstances. Raids of the Midianites on Israel warded off by Gideon (Judges 6:7) probably were those of nomadic tribes seeking escape from lands affected by moderate droughts. The second was a more massive migration during more extreme hot dry phases when farming populations were forced to desert their territories and move to areas with more favorable climates or where stable freshwater supplies were available. Collapse of the Akkadian Empire resulted from movement of Intermediate Bronze age people (4200 to 3900 B.P.) from north Mesopotamia into irrigated lands of lower Mesopotamia and lower Egypt. Migration of the twelve tribes of Israel from Canaan into Egypt is another example. The third large migration was evacuation of north Asiatic–European prairies because of deterioration of climate during Climatic Wet Phase III when grazing and farming ceased because of less solar radiation. These people were forced to move into climatically milder territories, pushing away less aggressive inhabitants and triggering a chain reaction of migration to the south. The movement of semitic Hyksos people to Egypt from northeast Mediterranean regions during Middle Bronze II was the end result. The rule of Hyksos over Egypt lasted 140 years, from 3700 to 3560 B.P.

In the Late Bronze age the Sea People—the Philistines and northeast Mediterranean–Asiatic people—unsuccessfully attempted to reconquer Egypt by sea and land invasions. The result of these adventures was the settling of Canaan by both Israelites and Philistines. During that time Egypt was temporarily weakened during an inverse relationship of wet and dry conditions between the middle latitude of the north hemisphere and the Sahara-Ethiopia belt. Reduced supply of water through the Nile River occurred at the same time of wet phases farther north in the Mideast region.

Correlation of Early Biblical History, Physical Data, and Archaeology

Rast's correlation of the Sodom tradition's time and locus with the Early Bronze age and within the Dead Sea south basin puts the Sodom and Gomorrah tectonic-seismic event at about 4350 B.P. If this date is correct, the time of the three patriarchs, Abraham, Isaac, and Jacob, must have been within about 200 years of Early Bronze III and the Intermediate Bronze age or between 4400 and 4200 B.P. Oral traditions of the catastrophic Sodom and Gomorrah event and subsequent association of back-and-forth migrations to Egypt enforced by repetitive droughts agree with increasing intensity of dry climatic conditions through these two cultural ages. Perhaps the extreme dry climate of Intermediate Bronze age correlates with migration of Hebrews to Egypt. During this same dry time, Nile floods must have increased as the monsoonal belt moved north and augmented precipitation over the Ethiopian and central Africa plateaus. That change could have corresponded with strengthening of Egypt during the Intermediate Bronze age relative to neighboring nations in the north. During Wet Phase III that followed, the Hyksos, forced to migrate south from north Levant along the coastal zone of the east Mediterreanean Sea, first invaded Canaan and then conquered Egypt. This movement was a demographic reaction to south migration of Asiatic people.

The long stay of the Hebrews in Egypt—first as tolerated, perhaps even helpful, guests until 3900 B.P. and then as a burden—may also be explained in terms of intensity of Nile floods. A decrease in fertility of the floodplain and delta may have been simultaneous with Climatic Wet Phase III. The Exodus of the Israelites which probably began sometime within the Late Bronze age could have included a stay of about 1,000 years in Goshen and was completed about 3200 B.P.

Increased precipitation over the north part of the Sinai Desert may have extended long enough to enable the wandering of fugitive tribes of Israelites together with their flocks across the Sinai and along the fringe of the Edom, Moab, and Ammon deserts. Confusion of governing systems may have occurred first in Canaan because of the increasing effects of droughts during the Intermediate Bronze age. Afterward, during Climatic Wet Phase III of Middle and Late Bronze ages, famine did occur in Egypt when sources of the Nile River underwent droughts brought by a southward shift of the climatic belt system. That crisis may have precipitated the desertion of the enslaved people from Egypt.

Although the general timetable of climatic and demographic changes sketched here may be correct, detailed biblical reports of some events are not always reliable. There is confusion in dating some physical events like earthquakes, climatic changes, and resulting invasions and cultural breaks. The possibility of a military conquest of Canaan by invading Israelite tribes from the east as compared with demographic and cultural mixing between different Canaanite tribes is not clear.

Identification of the "five cities of the plain" was only partly solved; much of it still is enigmatic. Close proximity of the city of Sodom to Mount Sedom along the west fringe of the south basin is highly probable but precise position of the city itself still is unknown. Although exact locations of Gomorrah, Admah, and Zeboiim also are unknown, Gomorrah probably was near the city of Sodom within the Sodom plain. The latter two may be identified in the future among the four known Early Bronze sites along the east fringe—the tels of Numeira, Es-Safi, Feifa, and Khanazir. Evidence is in favor of placing the Early Bronze site of Zoar at Bab edh-Dhr'a during the time of the Second Temple and of Byzantine, Early Moslem to Crusader cultures. Locating the satellite settlements of Mekhoza and Mazra'a along the south fringes of the Bay of Mazra'a is more convincing than in other geographical sites. The same holds true with respect to the Zered River and the route of the wandering Israelites during Exodus along the fringe of the east Jordanian desert.

Bibliography

Adams, J. 1982. Paleoseismology: A search for ancient earthquakes in Puget Sound. *Science* 258: 1592–93.

Aharoni, Y. 1964a. Mezad Gozal. *Israel Exploration Journal* 14: 112–13.

Aharoni, Y. 1964b. *Carta's Atlas of the Bible.* Jerusalem, Carta. 173 maps.

Aizenshtat, Z., I. Mileslavski, and E. Tannenbaum. 1986. Thermal behavior of immature asphalts and related kerogens. *Organic Chemistry* 10: 537–46.

Albright, W. F. 1924. The archaeological results of an expedition to Moab and the Dead Sea. *Biblical Association—Bulletin of the American Schools of Oriental Research* 14: 2–12.

Albright, W. F. 1962. The chronology of Middle Bronze I (Early Bronze–Middle Bronze). *Bulletin of the American Schools of Oriental Research* 168: 36–42.

Albright, W. F. 1965. *The Archaeology of Palestine* (Hebrew translation by A. Amir). Tel Aviv, Am-Oved Publishers.

Albright, W. F., J. L. Kalso, and T. J. Palin. 1944. Early Bronze pottery from Bab edh-Dhr'a in Moab. *Biblical Association—Bulletin of the American Schools of Oriental Research* 95: 3–10.

Allegro, J. M. 1958. *The Dead Sea Scrolls.* Baltimore, Penguin.

Almog, Y., and B. Z. Eshel. 1949. *The Sedom District: Zoar, the Dead Sea and the Plain* (in Hebrew). Tel Aviv, Hakibutz Hameuchad Publishing House.

Alt, A. 1989. *Essays on Old Testament, History and Religion.* England, Sheffield Academic Press.

Ambraseys, N. N. 1971. Value of historical records of earthquakes. *Nature* 232: 375.

Ambraseys, N. N. 1978. Studies in historical seismicity and tectonics. In W. C. Brice (ed.), *The Environmental History of the Near and Middle East since the Last Ice Age.* New York, Academic Press, pp. 185–210.

Amiran, D. H. K. 1991. The climate of the ancient Near East: The early third millennium BC in the northern Negev of Israel. *Erdkunde* 45: 153–61.

Amiran, R. 1977. Pottery from a Chalcolithic site near Tel Delhamiya and some notes on the character of the Chalcolithic–Early Bronze I transition (in Hebrew). *Eretz-Israel* 13 (Moshe Stekelis Memorial Volume): 48–56.

Amiran, R. 1986. The fall of the Early Bronze Age II city of Arad. *Israel Exploration Journal* 36: 74–76.

Amiran, R., and R. Gophna. 1989. Urban Canaan in the Early Bronze II and III periods—emergence and structure. In P. R. de Miroschedji (ed.), *L'urbanisation de la Palestine à l'age du Bronze Ancien: Actes du Colloque de Emmaus, 20–24 Octobre 1986*. British Archaeological Reports, International Series, 527, no. 1, pp. 109–16.

Amiran, R., and M. Kochavi. 1985. Eretz-Israel by the end of the third millenium—an intrusive culture or the last stage of the Early Bronze Age? (in Hebrew). *Eretz Israel* 18: 361–65.

Anati, D. A., and M. Stiller. 1991. The post-1979 thermohaline structure of the Dead Sea and the role of double-diffusion mixing. *Limnology and Oceanography* 36: 342–54.

Arieh, E., and Y. Rotstein. 1985. A note on the seismicity of Israel (1900–1982). *Bulletin of the Seismological Society of America* 75: 881–87.

Ashbel, D. 1951. *Bio-climatic Atlas of Israel and the Near East*. Jerusalem, Hebrew University Meteorological Department.

Avi-Yonah, M. 1953. *The Madaba Mosaic Map*. Jerusalem, Israel Exploration Society.

Avner, U. 1990. Ancient agricultural settlement and religion in the Uvda Valley in southern Israel. *Biblical Archaeologist*, September: 125–41.

Baney, R. E. 1962. *Search for Sodom and Gomorrah*. Kansas City, Christian Approach Mission Press.

Bar-Adon, P. 1956. Zinnabri and Beth Yerah in view of ancient sources and archaeological findings (in Hebrew). *Eretz-Israel* 4: 50–56.

Bar-Adon, P. 1957. Beth Yerah (Excavations, 1951) (in Hebrew). *Department of Antiquities, Bulletin* 5–6: 29–30.

Bar-Adon, P. 1977. Another settlement of the Judean Desert Sect at Ein el-Ghuweir on the shores of the Dead Sea. *Biblical Association—Bulletin of the American Schools of Oriental Research* 227: 1–25.

Bar-Nahmanni, Rabbi Samuel. 426–500. Midrash Rabba, assembled in A.D. 426–500: A comment on Jericho. In *Commentaries on the Pentateuch, Numbers XI*, 15, p. 657. Translated into English by J. J. Slotki, 1939, London, Soncino Press, p. 882.

Bar-Yosef, O. 1987. Prehistory of the Jordan rift. *Israel Journal of Earth Science* 36: 107–19.

Bar-Yosef, O., and E. Mintz. 1979. Epipaleolithic and Neolithic Industries. In A. Horowitz (ed.), *The Quaternary of Israel*. New York, A comment on Jericho: New York, Academic Press, pp. 307–19.

Bartov, Y. 1971. Strike-slip faults across central Sinai (in Hebrew). In *Israel Geological Society Annual Meeting*, pp. 5–8.

Bartov, Y. 1974. A structural and paleogeographical study of the central Sinai faults and domes (in Hebrew). Doctoral dissertation, Jerusalem, Hebrew University.

Begin, Z. B. 1974. *The Geological Map of Israel, 1: 50,000, sheet 9-III, Jericho.* Jerusalem, Geological Survey of Israel (Mapping Division).

Begin, Z. B., A. Ehrlich, and Y. Nathan. 1974. *Lisan Lake, the Pleistocene Precurser of the Dead Sea.* Jerusalem, Geological Survey of Israel, Bulletin 63.

Begin, Z. B., Y. Nathan, and A. Ehrlich. 1980. Stratigraphy and facies distribution in the Lisan Formation: New evidence from the area south of the Dead Sea, Israel. *Israel Journal of Earth Science* 24: 182–89.

Ben-Arieh, Y. 1965. *The Central Jordan Valley* (in Hebrew). Tel Aviv, Hakibutz Hameuchad Publishing House.

Ben-Avraham, Z., R. Hanel, and G. Assaf. 1977. The thermal structure of the Dead Sea. *Limnology and Oceanography* 22: 1076–78.

Ben-Avraham, Z., T. M. Niemi, D. Neev, J. K. Hall, and Y. Levy. 1993. Distribution of Holocene sediments and neotectonics in the deep north basin of the Dead Sea. *Marine Geology* 113: 219–31.

Ben-Menahem, A. 1981. Variations of slip and creep along the Levant rift over the past 4500 years. *Tectonophysics* 80: 183–97.

Ben-Menahem, A., E. Aboodi, M. Vered, and R. L. Kovach. 1977. Rate of seismicity of the Dead Sea region over the past 4000 years. *Physics of the Earth and Planetary Interiors* 14: 17–27.

Bender, F. 1974. Geology of Jordan. In H. J. Martini (ed.), *Contributions to the Regional Geology of the Earth.* Berlin, Gebrüder Borntraeger.

Bentor, Y. K. 1960. Israel. In L. Dubertret (ed.), *Lexique Stratigraphique International, Asie, 10c2: Congres Geologique International-Stratigraphie, Centre National Research Scientifique,* vol. 3.

Bentor, Y. K. 1961. Some geochemical aspects of the Dead Sea and the question of its age. *Geochimica et Cosmochimica Acta* 25: 239–60.

Bentor, Y. K. 1989. Geological events in the Bible. *Terra Nova* 1: 326–38.

Bentor, Y. K., and A. Vroman. 1957. *The Geological Map of Israel 1: 100,000, Arava Valley (with Explanatory Notes).* Jerusalem, Government Printer, sheet 19.

Berger, W. H., and L. D. Labeyrie. 1987. Abrupt climate change—an introduction. In W. H. Berger and L. D. Labeyrie (eds.), *Abrupt Climatic Changes.* Dordrecht, D. Reidel, pp. 3–22.

Beyth, M. 1980. Recent evolution and present stage of Dead Sea brines. In A. Nissenbaum (ed.), *Hypersaline Brines and Evaporitic Environments.* Amsterdam, Elsevier, pp. 155–65.

Blanckenhorn, M. 1898. *Das Tote Meer und der Untergang von Sodom and Gomorrah.* Berlin, Dietrich Reimer.

Bloch, M. R. 1962. Red salt and gray salt. *Mada* 6, no. 4: 3–8.

Bortenschlager, S. 1982. Chronostratigraphic subdivisions of the Holocene in the Alps. In J. Mangerud, H. J. B. Birks, and K. D. Jäger (eds.), *Chronostratigraphic Subdivisions of the Holocene: Striae.* 16: 75–79.

Bowman, D. 1992. Maximum altitude of the Lisan stage reevaluated: Ben Gurion University of the Negev, Bersheva, Geomorphological Meeting, pp. 35–36.

Braslavy, Y. 1956. *Around the Dead Sea* (in Hebrew). Tel Aviv, Hakibutz Hameuchad Publishing House.

Broshi, M. 1990. Agriculture and economy in Roman Judea (Erez Israel), according to Babta's papyri. *Zion, Israel Historical Society Quarterly* 55: 269–81.

Charlesworth, J. K. 1957. *The Quaternary Era with Special Reference to Its Glaciation.* London, Edward Arnold, 2 vols.

Clapp, F. G. 1936. Geology and bitumens of the Dead Sea area, Palestine and Transjordan. *American Association of Petroleum Geologists Bulletin* 20: 881–909.

Connan, J., and D. Dessort. 1991. Bitumen in balms of Egyptian mummies (1,295 B.C.–300 A.D.): Origin and quantitative evaluation. *Comptes Rendus Academie Science Paris*, ser. 2, 312: 1445–52.

Connan, J. A. Nissenbaum, and D. Dessort. 1992. Molecular archaeology: Export of Dead Sea asphalt to Canaan and Egypt in the Chalcolithic–Early Bronze age (4th–3rd millennium B.C.). *Geochimica et Cosmochimica Acta* 56: 2743–59.

Dan, J. 1981. Soils of the Arava Valley. In J. Dan, R. Gerson, H. Koyumdjisky, and D. H. Yaalon (eds.), *Aridic Soils in Israel*. Israel, Volcani Center, Special Publication 190, pp. 297–342.

de Vaux, R. 1973. *Archaeology of the Dead Sea Scrolls*. The Schweich Lectures of the British Academy. London, Oxford University Press.

Donahue, J. 1980. Geology. In W. E. Rast and R. T. Schaub (eds.), *Preliminary Report of the 1979 Expedition of the Dead Sea Plain, Jordan. Bulletin of the American Schools of Oriental Research* 240: 47–52.

Donahue, J. 1981. Geologic investigations at Early Bronze sites. In W. E. Rast, and R. T. Schaub (eds.), *An Interim Report of the 1977 Season: The Southeastern Dead Sea Plain Expedition. Annual of the American Schools of Oriental Research* 46: 137–54.

Donahue, J. 1985. Hydrologic and topographic change during and after Early Bronze occupation at Bab edh-Dhr'a. In A. Hadidi (ed.), *Studies in the History and Archaeology of Jordan*. Amman, Department of Antiquities, 2: 131–40.

Dor, I., and A. Ehrlich. 1987. The effects of salinity and temperature gradients on the distribution of littoral microalgae in experimental solar ponds, Dead Sea area, Israel. *Marine Ecology* 8: 193–205.

Dor, I., and N. Paz. 1989. Temporal and spatial distribution of mat microalgae in the experimental solar ponds, Dead Sea area, Israel. In Y. Cohen and E. Rosenberg (eds.), *Microbial Mats*. Washington, D.C., American Society for Microbiology, pp. 114–22.

Druckman, Y., M. Margaritz, and A. Sneh. 1987. The shrinking of Lisan Lake, as reflected by the diagenesis of its marginal oolite deposits. *Israel Journal of Earth Science* 36: 101–6.

Dubertret, L., and M. Dunand. 1954–55. Les gisements ossiferes de Khirbet El-Umbachi et de Hebariye (Safa). *Les Annales Archaeologiques de Syrie* 4–5: 8–76.

Ehrlich, A., and D. Noel. 1988. Sedimentation pattern in the Pleistocene Lisan Lake, precursor of the Dead Sea: New data from nannofacies analysis and the diatom floras. *Cahiers de Micropaleontology* 3, no. 3: 5–21.

Eisenberg, E. 1993. Sha'ar-HaGolan—The Middle Bronze I Site. In M. Stern (ed.), *The New Encyclopedia of Archaeological Excavations in the Holy Land*. Jerusalem, Israel Exploration Society, pp. 1342–43, 1548–50.

Emery, K. O. 1969. *A Coastal Pond Studied by Oceanographic Methods*. New York, American Elsevier.

Emiliani, C. 1978. The cause of the ice ages. *Earth and Planetary Science Letters* 37: 349–52.

Encyclopaedia Hebraica. 1955. The Epics of Gilgamesh. In *Encyclopaedia Hebraica*. Tel Aviv, Encyclopaedia Publ. Co., 10: 776–78.

Encyclopaedia Hebraica. 1960. Hieronymous. In *Encyclopaedia Hebraica*. Tel Aviv, Encyclopaedia Publishing Co., 14: 30–34.

Encyclopaedia Hebraica. 1961. Hunni (the Huns). In *Encyclopaedia Hebraica*. Tel Aviv, Encyclopaedia Publishing Co., 13: 883–86.

Esse, D. L. 1982. Beyond Subsistence; Beth Yerah and Northern Palestine in the Early Bronze Age. Ph.D. dissertation, University of Chicago, Department of Near East Languages and Civilizations.

Esse, D. L. 1989. Secondary state formation and collapse in Early Bronze age, Palestine. In P. R. de Miroschedji (ed.), *L'urbanisation de la Palestine a l'age du Bronze Ancien: Actes du colloque d'Emmaus, 20–24 Octobre 1986*. British Archaeological Reports, International Series 527, pp. 81–96.

Even-Shoshan, A. 1966–70. *The New (Hebrew) Dictionary*. Jerusalem, Kiryath Sepher Publishers, 7 vols.

Eyal, M., Y. Eyal, J. Bartov, and G. Steinitz. 1981. The tectonic development of the western margin of the Gulf of Elat (Aqaba) rift. *Tectonophysics* 80: 39–66.

Finkelstein, I. 1990. The Iron I in the Land of Ephraim—a record thought. In N. Na'aman and I. Finkelstein (eds.), *From Nomadism to Monarchy*. Jerusalem, Israel Exploration Society, pp. 101–30.

Fischer, H., H. Guthe, and G. Dalman. Undated. *Palestina 1: 700,000*. Leipzig, Die Geographische Anstalt von Wagner und Debes.

Folkman, Y. 1981. Structural features in the Dead Sea—Jordan rift zone, interpreted from a combined magnetic-gravity study. *Tectonophysics* 80: 135–46.

Freund, R. 1965. A model of the structural development of Israel and adjacent areas since Upper Cretaceous times. *Geological Magazine* 102: 189–205.

Frieslander, U., and Z. Ben-Avraham. 1989. Magnetic field over the Dead Sea and vicinity. *Marine and Petroleum Geology* 6: 148–60.

Frumkin, A., M. Magaritz, I. Carmi, and I. Zak. 1991. The Holocene climatic record of the salt caves of Mount Sedom, Israel. *Holocene* 1: 191–200.

Fuchs, V. E. 1947. The volcanics of East Africa and pluvial periods. In V. E. Fuchs, and T. T. Paterson (eds.), *The Relation of Volcanicity and Orogeny to Climatic Change*. Geological Magazine 84: 321–33.

Gardner, J., and J. Maier. 1984. *Gilgamesh*. Translated from the Sîn-lequ-unninni Version. New York, Vintage Books.

Gardosh, M. 1987. Water composition of Late Quaternary lakes in the Dead Sea rift. *Israel Journal of Earth Science* 36: 83–89.

Garfinkel, Y. 1990. Sha'ar HaGolan—1989 (in Hebrew). *Hadashot Archaeologiot (Explorations in Israel)* 95: 22.

Garfinkel, Y. 1993. Sha'ar HaGolan, Pottery Neolithic Excavations in 1989–1990. In M. Stern (ed.), *The New Encyclopedia of Archaeological Excavations in the Holy Land*. Jerusalem, Israel Exploration Society, pp. 1340–42.

Garfunkel, Z., and A. Horowitz. 1966. The upper Tertiary and Quaternary morphology of the Negev, Israel. *Israel Journal of Earth Science* 15: 101–17.

Gary, M., R. McAfee, Jr., and C. L. Wolf (eds.). 1974. *Glossary of Geology*. Washington, D.C., American Geological Institute.

Gasse, F. 1977. Evolution of Lake Abhé (Ethiopia and Terre Français des Afar Issas) from 70,000 B.P. *Nature* 265: 42–45.

Gasse, F., and F. A. Street. 1978. Late Quaternary lake level fluctuations and environments of the northern rift Valley and Afar region (Ethiopia and Djibouti). *Paleogeography, Paleoclimatology, and Paleoecology* 24: 279–325.

Gilat, A., and A. Honigstein. 1981. The polyphase history of the Qana'im Valley Fault Zone. Jerusalem, *Geological Survey of Israel, Current Research*, pp. 63–68.

Gilead, I. 1993. Sociopolitical organization in the northern Negev at the end of the Chalcolithic period. In *Biblical Archeology Today, 1990. Proceedings of the Second International Congress of Biblical Archaeology*, Jerusalem, Israel Exploration Society, pp. 82–97.

Ginzburg, A., and G. Gvirtzman. 1979. Changes in the crust and sedimentary cover across the transition from the Arabian Platform to the Mediterranean basin: Evidences from seismic refraction and sedimentary studies in Israel and in Sinai. *Sedimentary Geology* 23: 19–36.

Ginzburg, M. 1982. Life in the Dead Sea. *Israel Academy of Sciences and Humanities, Jerusalem, Section of Sciences, Proceedings* 20: 1–14.

Girdler, R. W. 1990. The Dead Sea transform fault system. *Tectonophysics* 180: 1–13.

Glueck, N. 1937. An aerial reconnaissance in southern Transjordan. *Biblical Association—Annual of the American Schools of Oriental Research* 18–19: 148.

Goldberg, F., and A. M. Rosen. 1987. Early Holocene Palaeoenvironments of Israel. In J. E. Levy (ed.), *SHIQMIM I studies concerning chalcolithic societies in the northern Negev Desert, Israel (1982–1984).* British Archaeological Reports, International Series, 356, no. 1: 23–33.

Goodfriend, G. A., M. Magaritz, and I. Carmi. 1986. A high stand of the Dead Sea at the end of the Neolithic period: Paleoclimatic and archaeological implications. *Climatic Change* 9: 349–56.

Gophna, R. 1979. Post-Neolithic settlement patterns. In A. Horowitz (ed.), *The Quaternary of Israel.* New York, Academic Press, pp. 319–21.

Gophna, R. 1992. The Intermediate Bronze Age. In A. Ben-Tor (ed.), *The Archaeology of Ancient Israel.* New Haven, Yale University Press, pp. 126–58.

Gordon, S. L. 1975. *New Commentaries to the Bible, Deuteronomy, 2:18–19: The Pentatheuh.* Tel Aviv, Masada Publishing House, vol. 1.

Har-El, M. 1962. *The Judean Desert and the Southern Dead Sea* (in Hebrew). Jerusalem, Sald Foundation.

Har-El, M. 1971. *The Judean Desert and the Dead Sea* (in Hebrew). Tel Aviv, Am-Oved Publishers.

Hestrin, Ruth. 1993. Beth Yerah. In M. Stern (ed.), *The New Encyclopedia of Archaeological Excavations in the Holy Land.* Jerusalem, Israel Exploration Society, pp. 255–59.

Hieronymus. 4th century A.D. Vulgate—Latin translation of the Bible. Munster, Sebastian, 1542, Isaias Propheta. [See Munster, 1542.]

Historical Productions. 1990. *1: 100,000 scale STM map (SPOT Landsat Space TM merge), Judea and the Dead Sea sheet, Cassini (Soldner) Grid Projection, 10 m pixels.* Tel-Aviv, Tal Publishing.

Horowitz, A. 1979. *The Quaternary of Israel.* New York, Academic Press.

Horowitz, A. 1992. *Palynology of Arid Lands.* Amsterdam, Elsevier.

Horowitz, I. Z. H. 1923. *Palestine and the Adjacent Countries: A Geographical and Historical Encyclopedia of Palestine, Syria and the Sinai Peninsula* (in Hebrew). Vienna, Harav Aharon Teitelbaum.

Ilani, S., and Y. Mimran. 1982. E-W trending mega-lineaments crossing Samaria. Jerusalem, *Geological Survey of Israel, Current Research*, pp. 42–44.

Imbrie, J., J. D. Hays, D. G. Martinson, A. McIntyre, A. C. Mix, J. J. Morley, M. G. Pisias, W. L. Prell, and N. J. Schackleton. 1984. The orbital theory of Pleistocene climate: Support from a revised chronology of the marine $\partial^{18}O$ record. In A. L. Berger, J. Imbrie, J. Hayes, G. Kukla, and B. Saltzman (eds.), *Milankovitch and Climate*, pt. 1, *NATO Advanced Study Institute*. Dordrecht, D. Reidel, 126: 269–305.

Issar, A., H. Tsoar, and D. Levin. 1989. Climatic changes in Israel during historical times and their impact on hydrological, pedological and socioeconomic systems. In M. Leinen and M. Sarntheim (eds.), *Paleoclimatology and Paleometeorology: Modern and Past Patterns of Global Atmospheric Transport*. Dordrecht, Kluwer-Academic Publishers, pp. 1–13.

Josephus, Flavius. 1906. *Antiquities*. In W. Whiston (trans.), *The Works of Josephus Flavius*. London, George Routledge and Sons.

Josephus, Flavius. 1959. *The Jewish Wars, A New Translation by E. A. Williamson*. London, Penguin Classics.

Kashai, E. L., and P. F. Croker. 1987. Structural geometry and evolution of the Dead Sea–Jordan rift system as deduced from new subsurface data. *Tectonophysics* 141: 33–60.

Katz, A., Y. Kolodny, and A. Nissenbaum. 1977. The geochemical evolution of the Pleistocene Lisan Lake–Dead Sea system. *Geochimica et Cosmochimica Acta* 41: 1609–26.

Kaufman, A. 1971. U-series, dating of Dead Sea basin carbonates. *Geochimica et Cosmochimica Acta* 35: 1269–81.

Kaufman, A., Y. Yechieli, and M. Gardosh. 1992. Reevaluation of the lake-sediment chronology in the Dead Sea basin, Israel, based on new $^{230}Th/U$ dates. *Quaternary Research* 38: 292–304.

Keller, W. 1957. *The Bible as History: A Confirmation of the Book of Books*. Translated by William Neil. New York, William Morrow.

Kenyon, K. M. 1979. *Archaeology in the Holy Land*, 4th ed. London, E. Benn.

Klein, C. 1961. *On the Fluctuations of the Level of the Dead Sea since the Beginning of the 19th Century*. Hydrological Service, Israel, Hydrographic Paper no. 7. Jerusalem, Ministry of Agriculture.

Klein, C. 1986. Fluctuations of the Level of the Dead Sea and Climatic Fluctuations in Erez-Israel during Historical Times (in Hebrew). Ph.D. dissertation, Jerusalem, Hebrew University Department of Geography.

Klein, R., Y. Loya, G. Gvirtzman, P. J. Isdale, and M. Susic. 1970. Seasonal rainfall in the Sinai Desert during the late Quaternary inferred from fluorescent bands in fossil corals. *Nature* 345: 145–47.

Kochavi, M., 1967. The settlement of the Negev in the Middle Bronze (Canaanite) I Age. English abstract of a Ph.D. dissertation, Jerusalem, Hebrew University.

Kochavi, M. 1973–74. A Middle Bronze I grave—a lined shaft—at Degania A (in Hebrew). *Qadmoniot* 6, no. 22: 50–53.

Kochavi, M. 1989. Urbanization and re-urbanization: Early Bronze age, Middle Bronze age and the period in-between them. In P. R. de Miroschedji (ed.), *L'urbanisation de la Palestine à l'age du Bronze Ancien: Actes du Colloque d'Emmaus, 20–24 Octobre 1986*, British Archaeological Reports, International Services, 527: 257–59.

Koucky, F. L., and R. H. Smith. 1986. Lake Beisan and the prehistoric settlement of the northern Jordan Valley. *Paleorient* 12: 27–36.

Kutscher, E. Y. 1974. *Words and Their History* (in Hebrew). Jerusalem, Kiryat Sepher Publishing.

Lamb, H. 1953. *The Crusades: Iron Men and Saints*. New York, Doubleday.

Lamb, H. H. 1971. Volcanic activity and climate. *Palaeogeography, Palaeoclimatology, Palaeoecology* 10: 203–30.

Lapp, P. W. 1968a. Bab edh-Dhr'a, Perizzites and Emim. In J. Aviram (ed.), *Jerusalem through the Cultures*. Jerusalem, Israel Exploration Society, pp. 1–25.

Lapp, P. W. 1968b. Bab edh-Dhr'a, Tomb A76, and Early Bronze I in Palestine. *Bulletin of the American Schools of Oriental Research* 189: 12–41.

Lapp, P. W. 1970. Palestine in the Early Bronze age. In J. A. Sanders (ed.), *Near Eastern Archaeology in the Twentieth Century: Essays in Honor of Nelson Glueck*. Garden City, N.Y., Doubleday, pp. 101–31.

Levy, Y. 1984. *Halite from the bottom of the Dead Sea*. Jerusalem, Israel Geological Survey, Report MG/48/84.

Lynch, W. F. 1849. *Narrative of the United States' Expedition to the River Jordan and the Dead Sea*. Philadelphia, Lee and Blanchard.

Macumber, P. C., and M. J. Head. 1991. Implications of the Wadi al-Hammeh sequences for the terminal drying of Lisan Lake, Jordan. *Palaeogeography, Palaeoclimatology, Palaeoecology* 84: 163–73.

Marmardji, A. S. 1951. *Textes geographiques arabes sur la Palestine*. Paris, Gabalda et Cie.

Mazar, B., T. Dothan, and I. Dunayevsky. 1966. En Gedi, the first and second seasons of excavations, 1961–1962. *Atiqot* 5: 1–100.

Mazar, B., M. Stekelis, and M. Avi-Yonah. 1952. The excavations at Beth Yerah (Khirbet al Kerak). *Israel Exploration Journal* 2: 165–73, 218–29.

McCreery, D. W. 1980. Paleobotany. In W. E. Rast and R. T. Schaub (eds.), *Preliminary Report of the 1979 Expedition of the Dead Sea Plain, Jordan. Bulletin of the American Schools of Oriental Research* 240: 52–53.

Melamed, E. Z. 1966. *The Onomastikon of Eusebius* (in Hebrew). *Tarbiz, Hebrew University*, 19 and 21. Jerusalem, Israel Exploration Society.

Milankovitch, M. 1938. Astronomische Mittelerforschung der erdgeschichtlichten Klimate. *Handbuch der Geophysik* 9: 593–698.

Mimran, Y. 1984. Unconformities in the eastern flank of the Fariá Anticline, and their implications of the structural evolution of Samaria (central Israel). *Israel Journal of Earth Science* 33: 1–11.

Mor, D., and G. Steinitz. 1985. *The History of the Yarmuk River Based on K-Ar Dating and Its Implication on the Development of the Jordan Rift*. Jerusalem, Geological Survey of Israel, Report, GSI/40/85.

Munich Reinsurance Co. 1986. *Earthquake, Mexico, 1985*. Order number 1080-V-e. Munich, Munchener Ruckversicherung-Gesellschaft, Königstrasse 107, D-8000, Munchen 40, Germany, pp. 32–34.

Munster, Sebastian. 1542. *Isaiah Propheta*. Hebrew, Greek, Septuagint and Latin texts. The two Latin translations are the 4th century Vulgate by Hierony-

mus; and the Munsteri, in which explanations of difficult Hebrew vocabu-
lary are from the commentary of David Kimhi. Basel, Henri Petrus.

Muzzolini, A. 1992. Dating the earliest central Sahara art: archaeological and
linguistic data. In B. Friedman and B. Adams (eds.), *The Followers of Horus,
Studies Dedicated to Michael Allen Hoffman*. Oxford, Oxford Books, pp. 147–54.

Nadel, D. 1991. Ohalo II—The third season (1991). *Israel Prehistoric Society Journal* 24: 158–63.

Nadel, D., and I. Hershkovitz. 1991. New subsistence data and human remains
from the earliest Levantine Epipaleolithic. *Current Anthropology* 32 no. 5:
631–35.

Nasr, S. N. 1949. *Geological Report No. 202 on Lisan Peninsula*. Amman, Transjordan Petroleum.

Neev, D. 1960. A pre-Neogene erosion channel in the southern coastal plain
of Israel. *Geological Survey of Israel, Bulletin* 25.

Neev, D. 1964. Recent Sedimentary Processes in the Dead Sea. Ph.D. dissertation, Jerusalem, Hebrew University.

Neev, D. 1978. The Geology of the Kinneret (in Hebrew). In Kinneret Administration (eds.), *The Lake and Drainage Basin—A Colloquium of Papers*.
Zemmah, Israel, pp. 15–26.

Neev, D., G. Almagor, A. Arad, A. Ginzburg, and J. K. Hall. 1976. The Geology
of the Southeastern Mediterranean. Jerusalem, *Geological Survey of Israel
Bulletin* 68: 1–51.

Neev, D., N. Bakler, and K. O. Emery. 1987. *Mediterranean Coast of Israel and
Sinai*. New York, Taylor and Francis.

Neev, D., and K. O. Emery. 1967. The Dead Sea. *Geological Survey of Israel Bulletin* 41: 1–147.

Neev, D., L. Greenfield, and J. K. Hall. 1985. Slice tectonics in the Eastern Mediterranean basin. In D. J. Stanley and F. C. Wezel (eds.), *Geological Evolution of the Mediterranean Basin*. New York, Springer-Verlag, pp. 249–69.

Neev, D., and J. K. Hall. 1979. Geophysical investigations in the Dead Sea. *Sedimentary Geology* 23: 209–38.

Nettleton, L. L. 1948. *Report on Gravity Meter Survey for Jordan Exploration Company, Dead Sea Area, Palestine*. Houston, Gravity Meter Exploration Company Report.

Neumann, J. 1991. Climate of the Black Sea region around 0 c.e. *Climatic Change*
18: 453–65.

Neumann, J. 1992. Climatic conditions in the Alps in the years about the year
of Hannibal's crossing (218 b.c.). *Climatic Change* 22: 139–50.

Neumann, J. 1993. Climatic changes in Europe and the Near East in the second millennium b.c. *Climatic Change* 23: 231–45.

Neumann, J., and S. Parpola. 1987. Climatic change and the eleventh–tenth
century eclipse of Assyria and Babylonia. *Journal of Near Eastern Studies*
46: 161–82.

Neumann, J., and R. M. Sigrist. 1978. Harvest dates in ancient Mesopotamia
as possible indicators of climatic variations. *Climatic Change* 1: 239–52.

Nir, D., and Y. Ben-Arieh. 1965. Relicts of an intermediate terrace between
the Ghor and the Zor in the central Jordan Valley, Lake Tiberias—Kefar
Ruppin (Israel). *Israel Journal of Earth Science* 14: 1–8.

Nissenbaum, A. 1969. Studies in the Geochemistry of the Jordan River–Dead Sea system. Ph.D. dissertation, University of California at Los Angeles.

Nissenbaum, A. 1990. Sailing routes in the Dead Sea. *Weizman Foundation Journal for Natural Sciences and Technology* 21, no. 10: 4–6.

Nissenbaum, A., Z. Aizenshtat, and M. Goldberg. 1979. The floating asphalt blocks of the Dead Sea. In A. G. Douglas and J. R. Maxwell (eds.), *Advances in Organic Geochemistry*. Oxford, Pergamon Press, pp. 157–61.

Nissenbaum, A., and M. Goldberg. 1980. Asphalt, heavy oils, ozocerite and gases in the Dead Sea basin. *Organic Geochemistry* 2: 167–80.

Picard, L. 1932. Zur Geologie des mittleren Jordantales. *Zeitschrift der Deutschen Palästina, Vereins der Vereinigung* 55: 1–169.

Picard, L. 1943. Structure and evolution of Palestine with comparative notes on neighbouring countries. *Jerusalem, Hebrew University, Geology Department Bulletin* 4: 1–134.

Picard, L. 1970. Further reflections on graben tectonics in the Levant. In *Graben Problems*, Proceedings of the International Rift Symposium, Karlsruhe, October 1968, International Upper Mantle Project, Scientific Report no. 27. Stuttgart, E. Schweizerbart'sche Verlagsbuchhandlung, pp. 249–67.

Pictorial Archive (Near Eastern History). 1983. *Historical Geography of the Bible Lands: Enhanced Satellite Imagery between East Anatolia and the Red Sea*. Vaduz, Leichtenstein, P.O. Box 34722.

Plant, W. G. 1981. *The Torah: A Modern Commentary*. New York, Union of American Hebrew Congregations.

Quennell, A. M. 1958. The structural and geomorphic evolution of the Dead Sea rift. *Geological Society of London Quarterly Journal* 14: 1–24.

Rast, W. E. 1987. Bab edh-Dhr'a and the origin of the Sodom saga. In D. L. Pardee, L. Toombs, and G. Johnson (eds.), *Archaeology and Biblical Interpretation*. Atlanta, John Knox Press, pp. 185–201.

Rast, W. E., and R. T. Schaub. 1974. *Survey of the Southeastern Plain of the Dead Sea, 1973*. Amman, Department of Antiquities of Jordan, the Hashemite Kingdom of Jordan, 19: 5–53.

Rast, W. E., and R. T. Schaub. 1978. A preliminary report of excavation at Bab edh-Dhr'a. *Annual of the American Schools of Oriental Research* 43: 1–32.

Rast, W. E., and R. T. Schaub. 1980. Preliminary report of the 1979 expedition of the Dead Sea plain, Jordan. *Bulletin of the American Schools of Oriental Research* 240: 21–61.

Rast, W. E., and R. T. Schaub. 1981. The Dead Sea expedition, Bab Edh-Dhr'a and Numeira, May 24–July 10, 1981. *Newsletter of the American Schools of Oriental Research*, no. 4 (1982): 4–12.

Rognon, P. 1987. Aridification and abrupt climatic events on the Saharan northern and southern margins, 20,000 B.P. to present. In W. H. Berger and L. D. Labeyrie (eds.), *Abrupt Climatic Changes: Evidence and Implications*. Dordrecht, D. Reidel, pp. 209–20.

Rosen, A. M. 1989. Environmental change at the end of Early Bronze culture Palestine. In P. R. de Miroschedji (ed.), *L'urbanisation de la Palestine à l'age du Bronze Ancien: Actes du Colloque d'Emmaus 20–24 Octobre 1986*. British Archaeology Reports, International, series 527, pp. 247–55.

Rotstein, Y., and E. Arieh. 1986. Tectonic implications of recent microearthquake data from Israel and adjacent areas. *Earth and Planetary Science Letters* 78: 237–44.

Rullkötter, J., and A. Nissenbaum. 1988. Dead Sea asphalt in Egyptian mummies: Molecular evidence. *Naturawissenschaften* 75: 618–21.

Rullkötter, J., B. Spiro, and A. Nissenbaum. 1985. Biological marker characteristics of oils and asphalts from carbonate source rocks in a rapidly subsiding graben, Dead Sea, Israel. *Geochimica et Cosmochimica Acta* 49: 1357–70.

Sakal, E. 1968. The Geology of Rekhes Menuha. Institute of Petroleum Research and Geophysics, Israel, report no. 5672. Master's thesis, Jerusalem, Hebrew University, Department of Geology.

Schattner, I. 1962. *The Lower Jordan Valley: A Study of the Fluviomorphology of an Arid Region*. Scripta Hiereosolymitana. Jerusalem, Hebrew University, Magnes Press, vol. 1.

Schuldenrein, J., and P. Goldberg. 1981. Late Quaternary paleoenvironments and pre-historic site distributions in the Lower Jordan Valley: A preliminary report. *Paleorient* 7: 57–71.

Schulman, N. 1978. Tectonics and sediments along the Jordan rift valley. In N. Schulman and Y. Bartov (eds.), *Jerusalem, International Congress on Sedimentology, Guidebook*, part II: 37–94.

Schulman, N., and E. Rosenthal. 1968. Neogene and Quaternary of the Marma Feiyad area south of Beth She'an. *Israel Journal of Earth Science* 17: 54–62.

Servant, M., and S. Servant-Vildary. 1980. L'environment quaternaire du bassin du Tchad. In M. A. J. Williams and H. Faur (eds.), *The Sahara and the Nile*. Rotterdam, A. A. Balkema, pp. 133–62.

Shaliv, G., Y. Mimran, and Y. Hatzor. 1992. The sedimentary and structural history of the Bet-She'an area and its regional implications. *Journal of Earth Sciences* 40: 161–79.

Silberman, N. A. 1992. Who were the Israelites? *Archaeology* (March–April): 22–30.

Steinhorn, I. 1985. The disappearance of the long term meromictic stratification of the Dead Sea. *Limnology and Oceanography* 30: 451–72.

Steinhorn, I., and G. Assaf. 1980. The physical structure of the Dead Sea water column, 1975–1977. In A. Nissenbaum (ed.), *Hypersaline Brines and Evaporitic Environments*. Amsterdam, Elsevier, pp. 145–53.

Steinitz, G., and Y. Bartov. 1992. The Miocene-Pleistocene history of the Dead Sea segment of the rift in light of K-Ar ages of basalts. *Israel Journal of Earth Science* 40: 199–208.

Steinitz, G., Y. Bartov, and J. C. Hunziger. 1978. K-Ar culture definition of some Miocene-Pliocene basalts in Israel: Their significance to the tectonics of the rift valley. *Geological Magazine* 115: 329–40.

Stekelis, M. 1992. Sha'ar HaGolan—the Pottery Neolithic A Site. In M. Stern (ed.), *The New Encyclopedia of Archaeological Excavations in the Holy Land* (in Hebrew). Jerusalem, Israel Exploration Society, pp. 1547–48.

Stiller, M., and Y. C. Chung. 1984. Radium in the Dead Sea: A possible tracer for the duration of meromixis. *Limnology and Oceanography* 29: 574–86.

Stiller, M., A. Ehrlich, U. Pollinger, U. Baruch, and A. Kaufman. 1983–84. The late Holocene sediments of Lake Kinneret (Israel)—multidisciplinary study of a five meter core. Jerusalem, *Geological Survey of Israel, Current Research*, pp. 83–88.

Stirling, J. 1954. *The Bible Authorized Version*. The British and Foreign Bible Society. London, Oxford University Press.

Street-Perrott, F. A., and R. A. Perott. 1990. Abrupt climatic fluctuations in the tropics: The influence of Atlantic Ocean circulations. *Nature* 343: 607–12.

Tannenbaum, E., and Z. Aizenshtat. 1985. Formation of immature asphalt from organic-rich carbonate rocks—I. Geochemical correlation. *Organic Geochemistry* 8: 181–92.

Tchernov, E., L. Ginsburg, P. Tassy, and N. F. Goldsmith. 1987. Miocene mammals of the Negev (Israel). *Journal of Vertebrate Paleontology* 7: 284–310.

Ten Brink, U. S., Z. Ben-Avraham, R. F. Bell, M. Hassouneh, D. F. Coleman, G. Andreasen, G. Tibor, and B. Coakley. 1993. Structure of the Dead Sea pull-apart basin from gravity. *Journal of Geophysical Research* 98: 21877–94.

Van Eck, T., and A. Hofstetter. 1990. Fault geometry and spatial clustering of microearthquakes along the Dead Sea–Jordan rift fault zone. *Tectonophysics* 180: 15–27.

Van Eysinga, F. W. B. 1975. *Geological Time Table*. Amsterdam, Elsevier.

Van Seters, J. 1975. *Abraham in History and Tradition*. New Haven, Yale University. [As quoted by Rast.]

Waisal, Y., and N. Liphschitz. 1968. Dendrochronological studies in Israel, II. In north and central Sinai (in Hebrew). *La-Ya'aran* 1: 2–22 (English summary, pp. 63–67).

Weinstein, J. M. 1984. Radiocarbon dating in the southern Levant. *Radiocarbon* 263: 297–366.

Weiss, H., M.-A. Courty, W. Wetterstorm, F. Guichard, L. Senior, R. Meadow, and A. Curnow. 1993. The genesis and collapse of third millennium north Mesopotamian civilization. *Science* 261: 995–1004.

Wetzel, R., and D. M. Morton. 1959. Contribution à la geologie de la Transjordanie. *Notes et Memoires sur le Moyen Orient* 7: 95–191.

Williamson, G. A. 1959. *Josephus Flavius: Antiquities and The Jewish Wars*. London, Penguin Classics.

Wright, G. E. 1961. The Archaeology of Palestine, in the Bible and the Ancient Near East. In G. E. Wright (ed.), *Essays in Honor of W. F. Albright*. London, Routledge and Kegan, pp. 73–112.

Yadin, Y. 1971. *Bar-Kokhba* (in Hebrew). Tel Aviv, Ma'ariv Book Guild.

Yechieli, Y. 1987. *The Geology of the Northern Arava Rift and the Mahmal Anticline* (in Hebrew). Jerusalem, Israel Geological Survey, Report GSI/30/87.

Yechieli, Y., M. Magaritz, Y. Levy, U. Weber, U. Kafri, W. Woelfli, and G. Bonani. 1993. Late Quaternary to Recent geological history of the Dead Sea area, Israel. *Quaternary Research* 39: 59–67.

Zak, I. 1967. The Geology of Mount Sedom (in Hebrew). Ph.D. dissertation, Jerusalem, Hebrew University.

Zak, I., and R. Freund. 1966. Recent strike-slip movements along the Dead Sea rift. *Israel Journal of Earth Science* 15: 33–37.

Zak, I., and R. Freund. 1981. Asymmetry and basin migration in the Dead Sea rift. *Tectonophysics* 80: 27–38.

Zertal, A. 1990. In the Land of the Perizzites and the Giants—the Israelite Settlement in the Hill Country of Manasseh. In N. Na'aman and I. Finkelstein (eds.), *From Nomadism to Monarchy*. Jerusalem, Israel Exploration Society, pp. 53–100.

Zielinski, G. A., P. A. Mayewski, L. D. Meeker, S. Whitlow, M. S. Twickler, M. Morrison, D. A. Meese, A. J. Gow, and R. B. Alley. 1994. Record of volcanism since 7000 B.C. from the GISP2 Greenland ice core and implications for the volcano-climate system. *Science* 264: 948–52.

Zilberfarb, A. 1978. Evidence for the Precambrian existence of the Gulf of Eilat fault zone. *Israel Geological Society, Annual Meeting, Proceedings*, pp. 44–46.

Zilberman, E. 1989. The Development of the landscape in the Central and Northwestern Negev in the Neogene and the Quaternary (in Hebrew, English abstract). Ph.D. dissertation, Jerusalem, Hebrew University.

Zori, N. 1962. An archaeological survey of the Beth-Shean Valley (in Hebrew). In *The Beth-Shean Valley: A Colloquium of Papers*. The 17th Archaeological Convention, Jerusalem, Israel Exploration Society, pp. 135–98.

Index